I0834062

With kind regards
of
your quondam chum
Archer Brown.

LOWELL LECTURES:

1871.

INSTINCT:

ITS OFFICE IN THE ANIMAL KINGDOM,

AND

ITS RELATION TO THE HIGHER POWERS IN MAN.

BY

P. A. CHADBOURNE, LL.D.,

AUTHOR OF "RELATIONS OF NATURAL HISTORY," "NATURAL THEOLOGY," ETC.

NEW YORK:
GEO. P. PUTNAM & SONS,
ASSOCIATION BUILDING.
1872.

Wm. McCrea & Co., Stereotypers, Newburgh, N. Y.

To

GIDEON L. SOULE, LL.D.,

PRINCIPAL OF PHILLIPS EXETER ACADEMY.

SIR,—I dedicate these Lectures to you with grateful remembrance of your counsels and instruction, and with sincere admiration for that scholarship and wisdom which, for fifty years, have done so much for the honor and usefulness of the Institution over which you preside.

With great respect and esteem,

I am most truly yours,

P. A. CHADBOURNE.

"But I see another *law in my members* warring against the *law of my mind*, and bringing me into captivity to the law of sin, which is in my members."—ROMANS, *chap.* vii. *ver.* 23.

"But mind this: the more we observe and study, the wider the range of the automatic and instinctive principles in body and mind and morals, and the narrower the limits of the self-determining, conscious movement."—HOLMES, *Autocrat of Breakfast Table*, p. 95.

"As dependent upon bodily organization, as actuated by sensual propensities and animal wants [man], belongs to matter, and, in this respect, he is the slave of necessity. But what man holds of matter does not make up his *personality*. * * * He is conscious to himself of faculties not comprised in the chain of physical necessity."—HAMILTON, *Metaphysics* (BOWEN), p. 16.

—"We can hardly find a more suitable expression to indicate those incomprehensible spontaneities themselves, of which the primary facts of consciousness are the manifestations, than *rational*, or *intellectual Instincts*."—*Ibid.*, p. 505.

"Now it may be that what we call instinct here, has not been sufficiently investigated. We hear men speak of the *higher instincts* and of *rational instincts*. Are these, then, for the higher nature what the lower instincts are for the lower? As many view it, *What is Conscience but a rational instinct*, a guide without comprehension, but rational, because it reveals itself as the voice of God, which all instinct is, without thus revealing itself?"—President HOPKINS, *Moral Science*, 1st Ed., p. 244.

CONTENTS.

LECTURE I.

INTRODUCTORY.

LECTURE II.

OPERATIONS IN INORGANIC NATURE AND PLANT LIFE THAT SIMULATE INSTINCT.

LECTURE III.

OPERATIONS IN PHYSIOLOGY SIMULATING INSTINCT; AND THE LOWEST FORMS OF INSTINCT FOR THE WELFARE OF THE INDIVIDUAL ANIMAL SUPPLEMENTING PHYSIOLOGY OR FUNCTION OF ORGANS.

LECTURE IV.

HIGHER FORMS OF INSTINCT FOR THE WELFARE OF THE INDIVIDUAL OR THE SPECIES, HAVING NO IMMEDIATE RELATION TO STRUCTURE OR FUNCTION OF ORGANS.

LECTURE V.

SOME MANIFESTATIONS OF HIGHER INSTINCT.—RELATION OF INSTINCT TO SPECIAL STRUCTURE AND FUNCTION.

LECTURE XII.

RELIGIOUS INSTINCTS.—SUMMARY AND CONCLUSION.

PREFACE.

SINCE these Lectures were written several important works have appeared that discuss many of the points here presented. It is proper to say that the outline of the Lectures was sketched in the Author's NATURAL THEOLOGY published in 1867; and many of the discussions are here abridged because presented with fulness in that work. In some places the discussion has taken the form of criticism of other works. This could not be avoided without ignoring many scientific and practical questions that are now topics of universal interest. Great respect is due to the opinions of those who have carefully studied any subject, but they are to be accepted only when borne out by facts. The necessity for independent investigation and thought is constantly pressed upon us by the fact that on many subjects discussed in these Lectures, the most diverse views are held by able men who have enjoyed equal advantages for investigation. Every observer and thinker may do something to settle these disputed points, but the scantiness of materials generally at hand and the liability to error in the interpretations of facts, should make every laborer cautious in his own work and lenient towards the mistakes of others. It is with a deep conviction of the need of the hearty coöperation of the cultivators of different fields of science, especially of Naturalists and Mental Philosophers, in the full study of man, that these Lectures are presented to the public. The necessity of investigation in special departments of science is readily conceded. But if men must consume all their strength on one specialty they should remember that excellence in that is no measure of their ability to decide questions in other departments. But such excellence in a single specialty, however restricted, is too often taken by its possessor and by the community as a measure of his just authority on every question he chooses to decide. Broad culture as a foundation for scientific attainments, respect for other sciences than our own and intercourse with those who view the same subjects from other stand-points than our own, are absolutely essential for safe generalizations in those complex sciences that relate to animal and rational life.

If these Lectures quicken the interest of any in the study of nature or in a more thorough investigation of their own complex powers, so that our relations to the world shall be better understood, they will subserve the purpose for which they were written.

WILLIAMSTOWN, MASS.
November 1, 1871.

INSTINCT.

LECTURE I.

INTRODUCTORY.

Investigations respecting the origin and destiny of man.—The central question.—Conditions of human progress.—Importance of Man's animal nature.—Comparative Psychology.—Power of Definitions.—Mistake in use of formulas.—Definitions of Instinct.—Vital activities to be traced.—Apparent work of Instinct.—Utilizes structure and function.—Includes impulse, knowledge, skill.—Natural History and Speculative Philosophy.—Man the perfection of the Vertebrate type.—Organs put to a higher use as the nature of the being demands.—Mind and thought.—Diverse philosophical views.—Works defined.—Results to be reached.—Topics for discussion.

"WHAT IS MAN'S ORIGIN AND WHAT IS HIS DESTINY," is the opening sentence of the course of lectures which I had the privilege of delivering in this place five years ago. This double question is still perplexing the world. Science is delving in bone caves, and peat bogs and lake deposits for records more ancient than historic books. Every split bone and fractured flint are interrogated respecting the customs of the early tribes of men, whose era upon the earth is known only by the geologic accumulations above their remains,—and whose manner of life is revealed only by the remnants of their feasts and the instruments of stone buried in the caves which their owners once inhabited. Every ancient human skull is measured—as to capacity and angles—to determine the animal affinities of man. Geology and history, sacred and profane, are scanned as never before—as eagerly as though the continued existence of the race depended upon the evidence which these records can give of the manner in which man came upon the earth and of the time when he came. Even those who profess to believe that it makes no difference to man how he came to be what he is, seem to have almost a mania for claiming bone caves as their ancestral mansions, and have little respect for the scientific attainments of any one who will not concede that the ancestors of all men were apes or gorillas.

Others as busy and eager quite, are peering into the future to learn what the race is yet to become. They sum up the advances made by man within the historic period, and especially within the last century, and then inquire, "What will the powers and opportunities of man do for him when he has numbered as many more centuries upon the earth as he has already numbered?"

Many generations must pass away before there can be any essential agreement among men who seek either for the origin or the destiny of man from the light of science. And so far as we can see, the past history and the future prospects of the race, if we are to depend upon science alone to reveal them, must always be like the bridge in MIRZA'S vision that had dark clouds resting upon either end. More and more of the span of the bridge may come into view to those who gaze upon it from the hill of science, but the abutments that mark the beginning of the human race, and its remotest future, will be in clouds and darkness still.

But there is a central question that relates to the present. WHAT IS MAN? If this question could be fairly answered, his origin and destiny would be in a measure deducible from the answer; or if it should throw no clearer light upon the past, it would reveal the goal towards which man must move, or the road along which his future course must lie in pressing towards that goal.

Amid all the din and clamor of science, which claims to give both the light and guidance which man needs as well as every other means of human progress, we wish to know what the HUMAN is,—what it has in common with the world below it,—what it has in its own right as its peculiar possession,—what there is in man to be ruled,—what there is in him having power to rule.

Again then we come to the task of analyzing human nature regardless of the sneers of those practical philosophers who talk of "the folly and heavy guessing of Metaphysics," grouping, as they generally do for their convenience, under this much abused term, all those studies that relate to the higher nature of man.

If we would improve man, we must know what

he is,—what powers he possesses and the law of their development. If he is a being of physical organization alone, let us understand that; and then give our whole strength to the study of physiology. If he has powers that are independent of the existence of this physical organization, something added to it, letus understand that. In fine, let us try to understand every power that man possesses, its use and the condition of its best activity.

Those who would reap most benefit from the laws of nature must learn what those laws are, and the methods by which variable combinations can work out new results, through invariable laws. The wise engineer while apparently contending against nature, always works with her and succeeds just in proportion as he obeys her laws. The wise philanthropist, or social scientist, will succeed in ameliorating the evils of society,—will elevate the race and secure its permanent progress, just in proportion as he understands the laws of human life, from its lowest manifestations to its highest, and labors to correct its mistakes by working in accordance with its own laws.

The laws of human life and its conditions of progress are as fixed as the laws of gravitation and cohesion. The errors and ruin of life arise from the power of man as a free agent to trangress those laws. It is in the sphere of the variable, where free personality through ignorance or perverseness, fails to supply the proper conditions of progress that we find the troubles of society; as in a fine piece of machinery, we find ruin when an ignorant engineer so arranges the parts that the power which should form the thread and web, rends and destroys the nice adjustments of the machine itself. If a machine is to do its full measure of work, its parts must so move that as little power as possible shall be lost in operating the machine itself, and its relation to the work it is to perform must be as direct and as accurate as it is possible to make them. To reach this result somebody must understand the machine. The same is true in regard to man. He is a machine of the most complex nature and he is also the engineer. Of all the exhibitions of ignorance in the world, the most common and the most disastrous in its consequences, is the ignorance of men of the right use of their own powers and of their relations to the work which it naturally falls to their lot to accomplish.

We recognize man first as an animal. Whatever higher powers may dwell in the body of man that body is animal in its orgin, life and death. The higher nature of man has for ages found diligent students. And the body has revealed to science both the structure and function of its organs so fully that almost every tissue and vital movement are known. The welfare of the body is now generally acknowledged to be a condition of mental power. But the animal life and animal nature have been too often ignored or undervalued in the study of man's higher nature. It has been deemed by some an insult to man to give him the instincts of the animal as the basis of his higher life or to assign them any high rank as instruments of human progress. And those who believe in the creation of man by a personal God have been slow to believe that He who took the bow in the clouds existing from the creation, as the appointed symbol of his promise to the race, has also taken animal powers in man and put them to a higher and nobler use than in any of the tribes below him. They need to study the great plan of God's economy in creation to learn that in each new form of life, nothing new is introduced until the possibilities of the old forms have been exhausted. The hand of man is no less wonderful or noble because it is foreshadowed in the fin of the fossil fish of the Silurian age.

As in the body of man we find the same sort of organs as in the lower tribes but fashioned for a higher use than such animals can need, so in his supersensual nature, we find the animal powers ministering to a higher life than those tribes ever possess. If there is a Comparative Anatomy there is also a Comparative Psychology. It is only when the comparison between men and animals is exhaustively made that we can reach that which is distinctive of man. If we can find nothing distinctive, then must we acknowledge him to be an animal in kind differing from the others only in degree. If we would escape from this admission, we must begin by granting to his animal nature all that belongs to it. When this is fairly done, what remains we may claim as distinctively human, with some hope of making good our claim.

In selecting INSTINCT as the subject of the present course of lectures, we take that which has been considered peculiarly the characteristic of the animal; but our work will all be in the service of man. We shall inquire into the nature of instinct, that we may trace with more clearness the operation of instinctive principles in our own constitution, and be able to give them their due consideration in all our schemes of education and social reform.

We meet a formidable difficulty at the very outset in the common forms of speech and in the scientific definitions of Instinct and Reason. A writer should use language in its common meaning if he can, and if he needs new words or new shades of meaning for old ones, he ought to explain his innovations fully and be consistent in the use of his new terms. But the best intentions and greatest care will seldom secure a writer from real inconsistency in the use of terms or from such a use of them that his meaning may not in some cases be misunderstood, even by careful readers. When words and phrases have had a fixed meaning with us, it is difficult to constantly give a different meaning to them. There is much error in the world that passes current, because it comes to us in well-worn formulas of speech, as counterfeit money passes among common people more readily when it has become soiled by the fingers of the hundreds it has deceived, than when it comes fresh from the printing-press. The very dirt and rents are marks of many judgments in its favor, and none but an expert would pronounce against the many endorsements of genuineness which it bears. It is to our mental gear not to say our moral convictions, like the shock of the suddenly stopping car to the body, for some bold innovator to demolish as baseless or false, some favorite definition—some good old form of speech in which our thoughts had run as in the track of truth.

But this power of language has its use. When truth has taken a particular formula of words for its expression, the formula alone will often answer our purpose; and we can use it, as does the mathematician his algebraic formulas, without the trouble of verifying them in every operation. It becomes one then who enters upon any investigation or discussion for the sake of truth, to guard himself at every step, lest he be misled by old formulas or by taking advantage of accepted formulas, cover error with them, deceiving himself and perchance those whom he attempts to instruct. If his object is simply to carry a point, the more he can bring his new doctrines under old forms of speech and his errors into the formulas that custom has stamped with the sanction of truth, the better will he succeed.

There is at the present time much controversy in the scientific world not only because men seem determined to confine the Baconian philosophy to matter alone, but because they insist upon using the same formulas for very different elements in the great circle of truth. The sine of ninety degrees is equal to radius, but the tangent of ninety degrees is infinite, and any mathematician who affirms that they are equal simply because they are related to the same sector of a circle, or tries to use the formula of one for that of the other, will waste his own labors and mislead all who trust in him. There is one part of the quadrant in which the tangent equals the sine of ninety degrees, and the formula of one might be used for that of the other without essential error. But after passing that point they differ more and more in value, until at another part of the quadrant no number is sufficiently great to express the difference between them. The change in the comparative value of these two elements is analogous to the divergence between the different elements in man's nature, that may, under certain conditions, be expressed by the same formulas, but which demand for their full treatment modes of thought and formulas of language widely different from each other.

As I propose to lecture on Instinct it might fairly be claimed that I should define the word at the outset. If I were to do so, few of my audience would agree with me fully. We should not agree where Instinct begins to control action nor where it gives place to another guide. Its nature and office would both be subjects of controversy. Were I to copy the best definitions ever written there is not one of them that some of us would not consider defective in some respects. It would either take for granted what we should not accept or it would deny directly or by implication what we are ready to assume as true. But we may be guided by these definitions, provisionally, treating them like bills before our Legislature, which may be altered or amended even to the "striking out of all but the enacting clause," and substituting entirely different bills in their place.

According to Paley, "*Instinct is a propensity prior to experience and independent of instruction.*"

Whately says, "*Instinct is a blind tendency to some mode of action, independent of any consideration on the part of the agent, of the end to which the action leads.*"

Hamilton gives this definition, "*Instinct is an agent which performs blindly and ignorantly a work of intelligence and knowledge.*"

Either of these definitions will serve a good purpose in guiding us in our investigation. We accept neither of them as complete. We shall make no attempt to define Instinct till the close of these lectures. And then probably instead of attempting a single, simple definition, as might be given of a single force or mathematical figure, we shall have to content ourselves with an enumeration of impulses and methods of action that are called instinctive, because they come neither from experience nor instruction.

We must assume that there is in the world something which we may call matter, force, vitality, sensation, voluntary action, Instinct and Reason. We will make no attempt now to draw the dividing line between them nor to determine how far one of them can be resolved into another. These may all be regarded, by some, as different manifestations of the same thing; but good usage of language demands of us, or at least allows us, to use these words as the names of distinct things and as terms so well understood as to need no special explanation, as they are used in this discussion. Their meaning, as generally understood, is sufficiently precise for our present purpose.

As it would be agreed by all that Instinct lies somewhere in the field of vitality, we shall trace that in all its manifestation, that we may find just what activities there are in the plant, in the animal, and in man. Throwing aside, if possible, our preconceived notions of the difference between them, we will inquire What they are? What they do? And before our work is done, we may be able to see whether there are distinct planes of being,—planes differing in kind,—or whether all manifestations of vitality merely differ in degree;—whether Instinct is something by itself as a distinct principle, or is a mere summation of powers acting in a specific method;—whether it is simply an extension of physiological function on the one hand, or the nebulous form of intellect and reason on the other.

The apparent work of Instinct, or the operation of the instinctive principles of action, is to fit the animal to the world; to enable him to battle for existence, to hold his place in spite of opposing forces and enemies,—in fact, to make the forces and products of nature his servants so far as they are needful for his perfection. It secures this by putting him at once, by a spontaneous manifestation of impulse, knowledge and skill, into the needful relations to those objects in nature that are necessary for his individual welfare or that of the species. It does this in many cases with almost the certainty of the operations of the laws of inorganic nature. Not more surely does the stone thrown into the air come to the ground, or water seek a level, than the bird knows its time for nesting and the material and fashion which mark the work of the species. And when Instinct varies or is deceived, as sometimes happens, it is done according to some law of the creature's being, by the introduction of some new condition ; as the stone returning to the earth may be turned from the curve which gravitation alone would give it, by the current of wind.

Instinct begins its work by utilizing structure and function of organs. Has the bird a gland for the secretion of oil? She knows instinctively how to press the oil from the gland and apply it to the feather. Has the rattlesnake the grooved tooth and gland of poison? He knows without instruction how to make both structure and function most effective against his enemies. Has the silk-worm the function of secreting the fluid silk? At the proper time, she winds the cocoon such as she has never seen, as thousands before have done; and thus without instruction, pattern or experience, forms a safe abode for herself in the period of transformation. Has the hawk talons? She knows by instinct how to wield them effectively against the helpless quarry.

But it is not structure and function alone that call instinct into play. There are certain manifestations of Instinct that are marvellous—manifestations that never could have been suggested to us by the study of the structure or function of organs. It is a function of the salmon as of the codfish to bring forth eggs. But why does not the salmon deposit her eggs in the salt waters where she loves to swim ? While the codfish finds her breeding place in the ocean, the salmon leaves the ocean and seeks the clear cold waters of the fresh streams as the place for depositing her eggs. She selects the best place in the stream, and after covering her eggs with gravel she leaves them to the care of the elements. She has done the best in her power for them and in all this work we say she is guided by Instinct. But in due time by the same sort of spontaneous impulse and knowledge or guidance, her young find the pathway to the ocean feeding grounds without the parent's aid. These are fair examples of instinctive action, or of spontaneous impulse, knowledge and skill, which are generally spoken of as the operations of some distinct principle in the animal.

The *impulse*, that arises in every one of the species at a given season of the year, or at a given period of its own development, to do the same thing—the apparent *knowledge* by which acts are performed to meet coming emergencies, the like of which the animals have never witnessed–the *skill* in working that comes without instruction or experience—all these are inscrutible. So much of all of these, as is needful for the preservation of each species, it seems to have as an original outfit, and that is all we can at present say. For convenience, we call this summation of spontaneous powers that extend beyond physiological functions, INSTINCT. This Instinct we find utilizing both structure and function. And we also see it making a broader manifestation controlling the whole being, as when the fowl hides from the bird of prey now seen for the first time, and the migratory birds and fishes know their appointed seasons.

In the manifestation of Instinct in the relation of the sexes—in the provision made by the parent insect for its young which it will never see—in the skill with which every organ is put to its specific use, with the same celerity and accuracy by animals of the same species from age to age, we find some of the most interesting fields of speculation. It is here that Natural History and Speculative Philosophy meet,—where they ought not to meet as opponents,—because if they do, one of them must be in the wrong,—but as allies in the search for truth, in unfolding the plan of creation, in setting forth its final causes and the varied relations of its parts.

But if Natural History and Speculative Philosophy are to meet on common ground and join as helpers in a common work, each should understand the other and not despise the materials nor the processes which the other is compelled to use. As to their materials, the two departments of science differ greatly. And in the clearness and precision of its processes, Natural History can certainly claim wonderful advances within a short time. This gives it the tendency to claim superiority and to challenge comparison. It is sure to come off victor, before those guided by the senses alone. For while great success has been achieved in providing materials for cabinets and in all fields of labor where the senses are the chief agencies employed, the whole supersensual world seems to be in a deplorable state of confusion to all, except to those philosophic minds who have the power to observe order in the midst of seeming chaos, and have also power to construct wholes from loose and disjointed fragments. The observers of the supersensual are comparatively few, and they are seldom young men; for the natural field of labor of the young lies chiefly in the region of sensible objects. There is therefore, in general, less enthusiasm and display among the students of mind and morals than among Botanists and Zoologists. There is in the study of the supersensual no method applicable for increasing the natural power of observation with such appliances as are always at hand for physical research and which so impress the multitude. Each observer is confined mainly to himself for his facts. The period of childhood he can explore only by the dim light of memory and by inference. In the whole realm of animated nature below him he now is, and must ever remain, entirely ignorant of sensation and will, except as he infers their nature from the study of himself and the comparison of himself with the lower orders of creation.

This comparison of the supersensual in animals and man should be more thorough than any that has yet been made and its results should be honestly accepted.

The comparison of man's anatomical structure with that of the lower orders of animals, has been most perfect and satisfactory. The whole vertebrate series is bound together with such homologies of structure that no casual observer even, can fail to recognize the unity of plan. A careful examination of the structure of man reveals not a single essential bone or organ that is not found in the lower members of the vertebrate group. If we take man as the perfection of the vertebrate type, then it is proper to say that every *essential* organ in the structure of the vertebrate animals is simply a modification of some organ found in man, either in his mature or early state. This comparison has been made so many times that the results are accepted as those products of science which no man of common intelligence is expected to deny. If there is doubt on any point, the materials are abundant for re-examination of the subject. Every bone, tissue and organ in the human body can be compared with the corresponding part in each one of the distinct vertebrate types within a year, by hundreds of men in different parts of the world. A new animal discovered can be compared with those already known and the modification of every organ be noted. This correspondence of bone and muscle seems to say that Creative Power seeks simplicity *through unity of plan*. He makes a hand, a foot, a wing or fin by the modification of the same organ, or more strictly upon one type. So fixed is this rule that if some vertebrate, such as had never before been seen, were to be now discovered, we should feel sure that its organs of locomotion, whether for running, flying or swimming, would be found to be fashioned on the type of the human foot and hand. But as regards the supersensual part in man compared with that in the lower animals, we find among the ablest students the most diverse opinions—some affirming that there is nothing in man not found in the lower animals,–that a dog even, has more moral nature than some men: and others of our able philosophers denying to man even the faintest manifestation of those instinctive principles of action that appear in the brutes. By some the brain is regarded simply as the organ of the mind, which as an incorporeal existence makes the brain its servant, as the engineer controls the engine, which may be broken, defective and even destroyed, while the engineer remains with all his capacities perfect. According to others, mind and thought if any distinction is made between them, are both the offspring of the brain—the result of the formation and decomposition of brain cells, the manifestation of forces evolved by a sort of higher chemical action, as heat is evolved by the union of coal and oxygen or the electrical current is set in motion by a certain interaction of metals and acids.

While among those who have studied man most carefully there is an essential agreement as to the facts of consciousness, in the metaphysical conclusions as to the nature of being, of mind and the mental processes there is the widest diversity. Nor are these speculations unimportant. They lie at the foundation of systems of education and morals. They influence us in training the young, and in our estimate of life; and they consequently shape the most important acts of our life. They will continue to influence the world in all its great movements of moral and social reform.

In a field where the thinkers are so divided, and where nothing but careful and long-continued observation, accurate analysis and cautious generalizations will avail, we cannot too soon begin the work nor prosecute it too zealously. If we are to reach correct results, we must here pursue the true scientific method of gathering facts and of fearlessly following the conclusion, which those facts warrants wherever they may lead.

It is generally conceded, if we judge from the language used by authors, that there is found in the animal kingdom, if we include man, *Instinct*, *Intelligence* and *Reason*. But when we ask, Are these distinct in kind or do they differ only in degree? Are brutes possessed of instinct alone? Has man instinct? What acts are instinctive and what are rational? The answers that come to us show that the best thinkers can seldom agree. In the majority of cases they differ not only in their statements, but when those statements are stripped of all possible ambiguity, it is found that there is a real difference in belief.

It is in vain for us to attempt to bring order out

of this chaos by definitions or by any mere accuracy of statement. Accuracy in language is impossible while the thought is confused. And definitions, if they do not correspond to the thing defined, are a constant source of mischief. The mind, satisfied with its definition, accepts that, and too often ignores the facts that ought to correct the definition, or misinterprets them to bring them into unison with some favorite system or theory.

Is it possible then to treat of Instinct without being misled by the word?—without being bound by some old definition that shall threaten us with destruction when we pass its limits, as the soldier is liable to be shot when he passes beyond the dead-line of his prison grounds? We will make the attempt. If we use any definition of Instinct, we will do it only for convenience, as we have intimated, holding ourselves free to search for facts and to give them an honest interpretation, even if they force upon us a new definition at every lecture.

Guizot has well remarked, when defining the word civilization, that it is the popular meaning of this word that we must investigate; and then adds, that the common meaning of a word is much more correct than the scientific meaning which has been given by a few persons under the influence of a particular fact that has taken possession of the imagination. The same is true, undoubtedly, of the word INSTINCT. It is the popular use of the word that must for the present serve our purpose as a name for certain phenomena as a whole, but it is Instinct as a *fact*, as revealed by these phenomena, that we must investigate.

It is our work then to inquire what animals do as sentient beings, as voluntary beings, as manifesting sensation, choice, volition, contrivance and memory,—to inquire how far an animal ever improves by experience,—in a word, to inquire what are the kinds of acts that animals perform and what are the conditions under which they perform them. Then we are to inquire what kinds of acts man performs and the conditions under which he performs them. When these two series of observations are placed side by side and a comparison is made between them, we shall have the best conditions possible for deciding what are the characteristics common to both man and the lower animals, and the means of detecting any power or faculty which either possesses as his peculiar distinction. From such an examination much might be hoped for, in rendering the lower animals more subservient to us and in securing to them proper usage; but its special use will be to give us a fuller knowledge of our own capacities and powers than could ever be learned from consciousness, or any study of man alone.

No attempt will be made to gather the wonders of Instinct, many of the accounts of which were invented or embellished for entertaining story-books; but the best known examples of instinctive action will be taken, such as can in most cases be easily observed in any part of the world, simply to show what Instinct is in its varied manifestations,—as a foundation for the comparison which we wish to institute between man and the lower animals.

If we mistake not, we shall find Instinct to be one of the great provisions which make the present condition of the world possible—an absolute necessity in animal life. It is one method of carrying out a plan, or if one objects to this phrase, it is one part of a great system which we find in operation around us. This system is a unity in its operations—so far a unity that we detect the same method in all its parts—in parts even the most remote. That we may see the relation of instinctive acts to other operations in nature and the use of Instinct itself, we shall trace the analogies of Instinct whenever we can find them. Our scheme then will embrace the consideration of the following topics,—

1. *The operations in inorganic nature foreshadowing Instinct.*

2. *The operations in plant life simulating Instinct.*

3. *The operations in animal Physiology simulating Instinct.*

4. *Lowest forms of Instinct for the welfare of the individual, supplementing physiology or function of organs.*

5. *The higher forms of Instinct for the welfare of the individual animal; as knowing its enemies without experience.*

6. *The relation of Instinct to special structure.*

7. *Instinct as necessary for communities of animals.*

8. *Development of Instinct by parental relation*

prompting the parent to provide for or to defend its young.

9. *Instincts of young animals to bring them into proper relations to their parents and the world. Also the peculiar instinct of one stage of being as preparatory to another in which that instinct is entirely lost,—as in the case of many insects.*

10. *Instinct of animals demanding certain changes in other animals or plants for the completion of its work.*

11. *Variation of instinct in domestic animals and its relation to man as making such animals useful.*

12. *Instinct as a law for the animal but subject to organic or functional changes in the system. Circumstances under which instinct may be deceived.*

13. *Higher character of animals. Do they think and reason? Have they intelligence as a guiding principle or subordinated to Instinct?*

14. *Instinct in man growing out of his appetites—wholly animal.*

15. *Instinct in its relation to the desires,—the basis of the social nature.*

16. *The nature of instinctive and intuitive knowledge.*

17. *Moral instincts. The distinction between men and animals and the directing power in both.*

18. *Relation of instinct to prayer, faith and immortality.*

19. *Relation of the subject to education, government and social reform.*

While this scheme gives the outline of thought to be presented it does not in all cases show the exact order in which the topics will be discussed. As the same phenomena appear in different departments of nature the same topics will appear in the discussion whenever the subject in hand aids in their illustration or needs them for its own. In such a field there is scope for the most thorough research and analysis. If we can but call more careful attention to these departments of study we may hope for much advantage to speculative science and practical life.

LECTURE II.

OPERATIONS IN INORGANIC NATURE AND PLANT LIFE THAT SIMULATE INSTINCT.

Definitions of Paley, Whately and Hamilton considered.—The office of the Physical Forces.—Life, Sensation, Volition.—Method of discussion explained.—Positivism.—Instinct part of a series of agencies.—Life depending upon the position of the earth and the changes within it.—Geologic changes.—Activities of the plant.—Instinct-like provisions of plants.—Community of action.—Special provision of the tree for itself.—Special structures and functions.—Provision made by plants for their young.

IN our last lecture we gave three definitions of Instinct from writers of acknowledged authority,—Paley, Whately and Hamilton.

Definitions might be multiplied, but those are as well fitted as any, for provisional use. Let us see exactly what they affirm. Paley says there is *a propensity prior to experience and independent of instruction.* From this we infer, that the propensity is to do something which might by some beings be learned from experience or that might be learned by them from another, by instruction. But we are not told whether the being that acts instinctively has any power of gaining knowledge by experience or from instruction, or whether it has any comprehension of the work which it performs. In fact the definition, instead of settling any thing, is simply a dogmatic assertion from which questions branch off in all directions. And many of our best naturalists would begin by denying the assertion altogether.

Whately says, *Instinct* is *a tendency to some mode of action*, and since he says it is a *blind tendency*—we suppose he argues that the tendency comes without experience or instruction. But he adds this important element to Paley's definition, that *this tendency is independent of any consideration on the part of the agent of the end to which the action leads*. Here then we have another very sweeping assertion, for it puts every instinctive act on a level with the movement of water under the influence of gravitation, or the movement of particles in the process of crystallization. This assertion is not made of certain instinctive acts but of all. According to this, whenever we decide that any act is instinctive, we must also decide that the animal performing it has no consideration of the end to which the action leads, however complex the action or wonderful the end secured.

This definition standing by itself without explanations would give rise to as much controversy as that of Paley; for after two men had agreed to accept it they still might be very far from agreeing whether a specific act was instinctive or not. After agreeing upon the definition, perhaps the first object seen would be a flock of birds migrating north. One might affirm migration to be with birds an instinctive act, and therefore that the birds had no consideration of the object of their long journey, while the other might believe that they went under the leadership of old birds that had learned, by the slowly accumulated experience of the species, where the best breeding places were to be found and therefore that the act of migrating is removed from the sphere of Instinct to that of Intelligence.

But both of these authors agree in this, that Instinct is simply a *tendency*. They do not speak of it as an existence, an entity, but as something like a *habit* though not gained by the individual by repeated acts, as habits are. It may be well in passing to say that there are able thinkers who regard instinct as nothing more than the fixed habits of the species, accumulated and transmitted after becoming fixed by long continuance.

When we consider Hamilton's definition we have a new element still. He says Instinct is an *agent*. If we understand this language at all, it implies that Instinct is an entity, something as distinct in existence as an element or as Reason, to say the least. And we are inclined to think that this is the common notion. We have frequent attempts made to draw the dividing line between Instinct and Reason, which implies that by such writers one is considered as much a distinct agent or agency as the other. Both terms however are often used in a very indefinite manner. But Hamilton adds that this agent, Instinct, *performs blindly and ignorantly a work of intelligence and knowledge.* Here we have again the assertion of entire ignorance on the part of the actor of the end in view in every instinctive act; but that the work is still one of intelligence and knowledge. We suppose this simply means that the work performed instinctively, that is, without a comprehension, by the actor, of the end aimed at, is such as would commend itself to the judgment of an intelligent and wise being as man may become by experience and by instruction from the experience of others. We must here anticipate our discussion by saying that we believe there are such acts, and that they have their place of necessity in the great system of means by which organic beings are kept on this globe.

If we commence with gravitation, the lowest and most far-reaching of all the forces that modify and control this universe, we can pass on through a series of agencies till we reach man, who has power of self-control and is able to comprehend the mechanism of the universe. And when he, through this power of comprehension, surveys all these agencies below him in their relation to each other, he finds each one of them doing, in its own sphere, just what Hamilton asserts to be the work of Instinct. That is, in their relations to other agencies, they are doing just what a wise being would approve of, because, by the combined action of all, results are reached that commend themselves to Reason.

It is gravitation that gives form to the globe, holds it in place and moves it as a part of a system of worlds around the Sun. Cohesion cements the elements together, gathers the minerals into veins, holds the continents in place, the mountains on their rocky thrones, and by its varying strength gives the different forms of matter upon the globe. Chemical affinity, with a magician's power, joins different elements to produce unnumbered products, and prepare the way for life. Life itself, known only in the development of some germ, answers to the call of the forces below it, and then in turn makes them its servants, till sensation is introduced. From sensation we have a whole train of reflex actions and the craving of the appetites that tend to preserve the organism but are involuntary in their action. Then one step higher we have acts which arise from spontaneous impulse, that are always dependent upon volition, and involve skill and adaptation of means to ends, but are apparently performed without any comprehension of the end, by the actor. One step higher still we have acts that originate from some spontaneous impulse but are plainly modified by some consideration of the end or some comprehension of the results. All of these classes of acts man can see below him. And these three classes of acts have been strangely mingled together in treating of Instinct. It is not strange therefore that there have been disagreement and confusion.

Most authors have started with some definition of Instinct like those given, and then have joined with it the assertion that the lower animals have no Intelligence. It is no wonder that they have found difficulty in drawing the dividing line between instinctive and rational acts, even using the word rational in its lowest sense.

All the agencies from gravitation to Instinct, as thus far defined, are parts of one plan, and they all do the work of Intelligence as much as Instinct itself; that is, a work that in the end is approved by man—the highest Intelligence on the globe.

That we may see that Instinct is nothing peculiar as to its method of action, we shall briefly trace the action of the agencies below it that are conditional for its work. And we therefore invite your attention to a brief examination of the first two topics of the program presented at the close of our last lecture.

The operations in inorganic nature and plant life that simulate Instinct.

It was the notion of some formerly that the earth was a living thing. The balmy breezes and the storms, the ceaseless tides that mark the changing level of the oceans, and the earthquakes rending the solid ground, were all the living movements of this huge Behemoth, the earth. This poetic notion has no place in the prosaic, scientific beliefs of the present day; though there was such a semblance of truth as its foundation, that much of its language and something of its impression still remains even with the most cultivated. In figurative language we speak of the earth as our mother, and there is significance in the language as we come from her bosom, enjoy the boundless provision which she has made for our wants, and then are gathered to her peaceful rest. But it is only in poetic language and by that power of association that makes a tree, a brook or the old farm-house dear to us as a friend, that we can speak of the earth as other than a clod. Through all this mechanism and the forces by which man is formed of the dust of the earth and his wants provided for, we may recognize the power, wisdom and skill of a Personal Being. We may do the same in the manifestations of acknowledged Instinct in animals and the affections in man; since they all form parts of a system and of such a system as the wisdom of man approves of—such as he cannot refer to chance nor to this clod of earth, with all its elements and forces. But all such questions as to chance, design, personality and its attributes manifested through the works of nature, belong to Natural Theology, with which we have nothing now to do.

For our present discussion we inquire simply for manifestations; and we do not propose to trace those manifestations farther than to the agent or being in which they appear. Our first question in every case will be, *What is?* not, *How came it so?* How is the earth, the plant, the animal and man constituted? Not, How came they to be so constituted?

For the purposes of our present inquiry we may believe that all things began to exist a century ago, or that they have existed for an indefinite cycle of ages. Questions of origin are proper subjects of investigation, but they have only an incidental bearing upon our present discussion. Such questions may arise in the progress of our investigations, but we shall not seek for them nor feel bound to attempt their answer.

Shall we then free ourselves of all preconceived notions of creation—of development, of Theology—of how things *ought to be*—or, at least, leave them for future discussion and apply ourselves to the task of learning *what is*—in the department of nature which we propose to investigate? If we can do this, we shall gain for ourselves all the good which Positive Philosophy has ever had to offer as a guide in science, without committing ourselves to its dogmas. And this much should be said in favor of Positivism, that its method is the only true one for approaching every natural science. Whether the human mind can stop, or ought to attempt to stop, within the limits which Positive Philosophy prescribes for it, is a very different question.

Will you allow me then, for convenience of language, to speak of the earth with all its elements, the stars and planets, as all acting by a power of their own to produce the varied results that are naturally ascribed to them? But these results ascribed to them are meaningless to us unless they have some known connection with an end. And an end or purpose either by itself or as part of a series of purposes, is always apprehended by us as having relation to sentient beings.

We recognize then in the operations of inorganic nature certain provisions for organized beings—beings that can grow, flourish, languish and die. The full provision consists of a mutual adaptation of the being and the world to each other. It is a maxim accepted almost without a dissenting voice, that animals provide for themselves by Instinct. Instinct seems to be regarded as something that has power to lay the world under contribution for its possessor's good. It has been considered quite too much by itself, rather than as a part only of that complicated series of adjustments by which living beings are kept upon the globe. How small a part it plays among the lower animals, and the rank of its work, will be best understood by understanding the whole machinery of which it is only one wheel—a part essential to the range of animal life upon the globe, but still utterly valueless were there not a more complicated machinery or more complicated parts of the same machine in constant operation. Instinct alone would be like the loom of the cotton-mill with no card or spinning-frame to prepare material for its work. It is in the inorganic world, in the vegetable kingdom and in the anatomy and physiology of the animal system that we find the supplementary parts of that nicely-adjusted machine which we call Nature.

The earth is clothed with plants, the rivers, lakes and oceans have their share of vegetable life. And rising higher still on the land and swarming in the waters, are the varied forms of the animal kingdom. We speak of animals as adapting themselves to the world by Instinct, and of the plants as finding their places by some law of distribution. All this is true. But the immediate agencies that attract our attention in both cases are only a part, and a small part, of the agencies that secure the result. How futile would be the keenest Instinct of animals, and how useless all the machinery in the vegetable kingdom for the distribution of plants, if the earth itself were not a preserver of both animals and plants by the balance of its forces and the ready yielding of its elements for their protection and support!

We cannot tell what compensations there may be on other planets to make such life as our earth has possible on them, or what forms of life may be fitted to flourish under their physical conditions; but the constitution of our earth we can understand, and the capabilities of all living forms both of plants and animals we are able to gauge. If we cannot mark the exact power of endurance of each kind, we can set a limit of cold and heat beyond which no living thing could exist. A nearness to the sun that should give us a temperature of three hundred degrees in every portion of the globe would render the existence of every known form of life now upon our earth impossible. A temperature of zero continued for ages would bring all oceans to solid ice, and in the end make the earth a barren waste.

Let the earth then wander from her path and approach the sun until she circles far within the orbit of Mercury, or let her forget the centripetal force and extend her path to the outer verge of the solar system; in one case she would become a blazing ball until wrapped in the terrible mantle of oceans changed to steam; in the other, earth and water would be changed to solid stone and the summer's cold would exceed the deadly breath of arctic winter in the depth of its polar night. How powerless every form of life would be under such changes! The adaptation of the plant, the Instinct of the animal, the forethought, the wisdom and science of man would be without avail, and all forms of life would as surely perish as the nestlings of the bird or the tender infant would perish without a parent's care.

The young bird just raises its head and opens its bill to be fed. Without the responsive care of the mother it must die. Little more than this act of the young bird, in the series of acts necessary for its support, is the act of the most cunning Instinct or of human wisdom itself compared with all the labors of mother earth to supplement their acts in sustaining life or securing enjoyment. The earth completes her circuit round the sun and gives each year the conditions of some form of life from pole to pole. She supplements, on a grand scale, the structure, function and Instinct of all the tribes that dwell upon her. No matter now how all these adjustments were secured. Structure and function and Instinct are adapted to the conditions of the globe, and all of these together secure or make possible the forms of life that now exist. And what a multitude of conditions must combine in the structure and movements of the earth itself to foster the wealth of life which she lovingly bears on her bosom! In the summer months she cares for the northern zone. She wakes to life the sleeping germs, the waiting buds and bulbs, by lengthening the day and wooing the vertical sun as the mother bird with patient watching warms to life the egg within the nest. But when the sun has quickened life, the office of the earth has but just begun, as the work of the mother bird begins in earnest when the hungry brood call for food.

The quickening of the thousand forms of life, from bud and root and seed seems the signal to the earth for renewed activities on every side to supply them with the means of growth. In the soil she sets to work a laboratory so wonderful that all the science of the world cannot equal the perfections of its operations. She there combines the gases, gives up the richness of her rocks and forms the food on which plants can alone exist. Then through the thousand pores she draws the food in contact with the rootlets that are eager to drink it in. In the air she brings to every leaf a supply for its thousand hungry mouths. At night she distills the refreshing dew, and anon she brings up the thick water cloud that, descending in the rain, gives verdure to the field and forest and springs among the hills. Who can contemplate the machinery by which life is sustained for a single summer and not be struck with the wonderful provisions in inorganic nature, a single one of which failing no adjusting power of animals or plants could save them? That chemistry of soils and air,—that mechanism of attraction,—that machinery of evaporation and transportation and condensation must all be kept in constant operation to secure this one result, the perpetuation of life on the globe. And how wonderfully alike is the sum of all these agencies from year to year!

The winds blow when and where they list—the days of wet and drought and heat and cold no one can foretell. But at the end of the year, the result of all these operations is found to be near the result for all other years—to come so near to the ordinary range of climatic change that it may with truth be said that seed-time and harvest never fail.

Nor is the earth's work finished when this complicated machinery within her soil and atmosphere has covered the fields and forests with their yearly fruits. When the plants have provided for themselves in ways which we shall describe, through this agency of the earth, she, like a careful mother, provides for their winter's sleep. In northern climes the water takes the feathery form of snow, and like a covering of down protects the tender plants and roots so that many forms are preserved that but for this protection would be destroyed or confined to more southern lands. While northern life is sleeping, the same forces that once acted upon it are providing for the southern zones. If we go back to geologic ages the lesson is the same. The provision was the same in kind as now appears, but each geologic age was itself a provision for those that were to follow—and all of them were preparatory for the present. While the earth supplied the wants of the tribes that held possession of her, in each of her unmeasured eras, she was providing as by a demiurgic Instinct for the present generations. No matter now what were the forces employed, no matter whether all this work is the wild sport of chance or the ordaining of Infinite Wisdom. In either case the result is plain, and such a one that all must admit that the structure of the earth and all its surroundings justify themselves to reason as a fit provision for such a being as man is. As he progresses in knowledge he not only does better for himself, but he discovers new adaptations of this physical universe to his wants. Every fracture of the rocks, every folding stratum, every vein of metal, every mineral deposit and every step by which oceans were bounded, mountain chains thrown up, water sheds determined, river channels cut and springs planted among the hills, all these labors of the earth, seem to have been as truly for her children—for every living thing—as the instinctive work of animals is for their young which they provide for, though perchance are never to see.

Thus far we have spoken of the earth as though caring for organic beings as the mother cares for her children. In all the changes of the earth there have been results that simulate the work of Instinct, and simulate it so closely that many changes in the inorganic world supplement the operations of life, as though the Physical Forces, Physiological Forces and Instinct took counsel together in caring for every living thing, and each took up the task at an appointed time. One responds to the other, and so completely do they do this that it is difficult in all cases to say which we should most admire in the parts they play in carrying on the work. As the young of the animal responds to the parent's Instinct to secure its aid, so do the various tribes of plants respond to inorganic nature.

In the changes of the inorganic world we recognize no care for itself. There is nothing in itself to be cared for. We see no purpose except in connection with life or in relation to it. And however vague our notion of Instinct may be, we always recognize in it some purpose, and that purpose as having relation to life. We may then readily recognize operations in inorganic nature having reference to plants, their preservation or growth, while there is no possibility of recognizing such care in the globe itself for its own sake or for the sake of any of its parts. We do not see how Infinite Wisdom even could devise any thing for the good of inorganic nature or any part of it. The conditions of receiving good are found only in living beings.

But in the plant, a living being, we may recognize a provision for itself, because in it is a life to be preserved, and certain conditions are to be secured for the best manifestation of that life. The plant also may have relations to the animal kingdom, making for it, or some portion of it, instinct-like provisions, as inorganic nature has made for the plant.

We have here also in the plant an entirely new field of activities—those growing out of real parental relation. The tree has not only to provide for itself but for the thousand young plantlets set free in its seeds, each one fitted to become a new centre of life and representative of the species. We have then in the plant all those activities that secure in the vegetable kingdom the same ends which in the animal kingdom are usually secured by Instinct—care of the individual and the production and care of young for the preservation of the species. For convenience in illustrating these activities we shall speak of the plant as sentient.

The curious processes by which every species adapts itself to the world may be structural or functional; but a plan is so readily recognized and the results are reached by such complicated operations, all moving harmoniously together, that every observer must be struck with the close imitation of voluntary action—of instinctive foresight and skill in adapting means to ends. We have this apparent foresight and skill manifested to some extent in almost every plant that clothes the earth, and almost every species has manifestations of contrivance peculiar to itself.

The study of the instinct-like provisions in the growth of plants and bodies of animals will prepare us to understand that acknowledged Instinct, in its lowest forms, simply carries the work of life one step farther through volition, than mere structure and function could possibly do.

The best known trees—the oak or apple—will afford ample illustration of provisions for themselves and young that simulate the work of Instinct.

The oak, that must brave the storms for centuries, sends out its thickened roots swelling high from the trunk, like buttresses to a castle wall, but firmer in position and better balanced than any ever fashioned by the wisest architect. The Eddystone light-house, that defies the power of the sea, was fashioned by its great builder, Smeaton, from the study of the oak. Well may this tree be taken as the symbol of strength. Every limb is banded with swollen rings of gnarled and knotted fibre. The work is done for centuries, and every year adds new supports to meet the increasing weight from growth. But this work is all varied as the exigencies of the case demand. The oak upon the hill-side, exposed to every wind, builds its base broader, springs every buttress deeper, and strengthens most the side that must bear the constant attack. All this is the law of its growth, says one. Certainly it is, but that law of growth provides, like the law of Instinct, for the preservation of the individual according to the conditions which are to be met. There is in the organism a certain amount of flexibility, enabling it to meet the varying conditions, and an actual change according to the conditions, as certain and complete within certain limits as though sensation and volition were agencies in the work.

Every tree is a community of individuals, and the trunk is the common work of all the buds and for their use, as the coral dome is for the coral polyps, or the hornet's nest is for the community of hornets. The coral dome is the product of growth and the nest is the work of Instinct; but they both have the same relation to a community, they are the joint product and the joint property of all the individuals that labored or were concerned directly or indirectly in their production. As the coral polyp, each working for itself, aids by the law of its growth to build up a structure for the benefit of the whole colony, so do the oak buds by the law of their growth build up the trunk and all the machinery of the roots for the benefit of the thousands of individual plants or buds that make a full grown tree. In the same way, but under the impulse and guidance of Instinct, do social animals, like the hornet and beaver, build nests and dams for the common good.

Since the tree is fixed to one place and yet must feed mainly upon the products of the soil, it provides for itself anew every year organs for feeding, by increasing its surface of root by the formation of fibrils that penetrate the soil in all directions. The food of the tree consists of the salts and gases in solution. As these substances are carried down by abundant surface rains, or drawn up by capillary attraction, they cannot escape the eager rootlets that sweep the soil in all directions by their fixed net-work, as completely as the coral polyp and other forms of animals sweep the waters with their tentacles.

In the spring time also the tree puts out its wealth of leaves to gather additional food from the air. And what ample provision is made for carrying on this work! What apparent forethought and wisdom do we here find in the economy of the tree! The leaf not only gathers crude materials from the air, but it is the laboratory in which all materials taken from both earth and air are elaborated and fitted for building up the tree in all its parts. The material that forms the leaf must itself be first elaborated. How shall the tree without leaves clothe itself with its acres of foliage? It does this by a foresight which closely imitates the higher provisions made by Instinct. Near the close of each season there is elaborated by every tree food that is not then used but stored up in its tissues for a day of need. That time of need is the next spring, when the new generation of leaves suddenly appears, unfolding as garlands of beauty upon every tree and shrub, but having in addition to their beauty of form and color for adorning the earth, the more important office of building up the tree and preparing for flowers and fruit that without the leaf would wither and fall for want of food. Now it is, as a first step in the work of the new year, that the material prepared beforehand by the tree and safely kept in its tissues during the winter months, is called into requisition for leaf-making. In vain would the spring sunshine and showers soften the sward and stimulate the buds, and quicken the roots to gather materials from the soil—the tree would die in the midst of plenty and with every outward condition in favor of its life, had it not wisely stored up material already elaborated for the making of leaves. When they are once unfolded, the earth and air are both laid under continued contribution to furnish all the products of the year. And when the layer of woody fibre has been added to the tree, the fruits brought to their perfection and the buds set and sealed with cunning workmanship, the tree lays by a store of food for the growth of those buds which are to enliven another year, as certainly as the instinct-guided animal ever made provision for its young.

This apparent forethought in preparing materials and storing them for a time of need, is not manifested by the trees alone, but in a greater or less degree it is exercised by every plant that grows—most manifest is it in those that live more than a single year.

What wonders are performed beneath our very feet! If we could look beneath the thick woven sward of the meadows, or roll back the decaying leaves of the forest, or pluck up the thickened rootstocks of the water lily and kindred forms from their oozy beds beneath the shallow lakes, we should find in every place evidence of instinct-like forethought among the plants and provision for their future wants.

When the frost of autumn and ice of winter have covered the earth with death, so that to the eye there seems to be but mere remnants of withered grass and herbage, we still wait in confident expectation that spring will wake new forms to sudden life from hidden germs, as by enchantment. In roots of grass and bulb of lily, in all the thousand store-houses beneath the soil, the busy, prudent plants have laid up their provisions ready for instant use—not to preserve life in winter—but for their spring's work in bringing sudden beauty of leaf and flower upon the earth, when wakened to activity from their winter's sleep. They answer to the call of the great magician, the sun, whose touch dissolves as by enchantment the flinty soil and palsying power of winter; and now with eager haste they utilize the stores of food which they carefully reserved the year before, when they seemed to be living to the extent of their means. There is no such foolish extravagance, in the plant economy, as living to the full extent of income each year, except when the time has come for the plants to pass away and then with true parental Instinct they bequeath all they possess to their children; which bequest is always found to be just enough to start the young plantlets well in life, till large enough to work and gather materials for themselves. All the wealth of beauty in early spring—the green blade of grass—the fragrant Arbutus of the hill-side and the golden Caltha by the brook,—these all are the products of plant labor of the former year.

These slow, secret processes are hid from the eye of the most careful observer, and they would never be known were it not for the sudden display of leaf and flower in spring time, that reveals the secret of this hoarded wealth.

But there are other processes by which the plant provides for its growth and seemingly for its enjoyment and rest, as though it were a sentient being. The Sun-flower turns its broad disk towards the sun that its hundreds of flowers packed in one head may bask in his light. A multitude of smaller flowers that fail to attract the attention of common observers, are silent worshippers of the sun, or turn fondly towards his life giving rays. And not the flowers alone but leaf and stalk bend from the darkness towards the light which can alone give the conditions of life and growth. The power that turns them is no mere enlargement of cells nor change of structure as we are sometimes told, but the movement is as inscrutible as the folding of the leaf of the sensitive plant, or the sleep of the water lily when she folds her petals of ivory and gold, to gather new beauty and richer perfume for the morrow.

There are among plants other operations whose purpose we may not be able to solve satisfactorily, while the acts or operations have all the characteristics of instinctive contrivance. What shall we say of the Catch-flies that at every joint pour out their sticky fluid that holds all the smaller insects as bird-lime spread by the fowler's art, holds birds upon the branch? There is also the Venus's fly-trap of our southern states, that has a portion of its leaves fashioned specially for its work—the barbs all set for holding their prey—the bait poured out by the trap itself to allure the unsuspecting fly within the cruel jaws that close all the tighter for the victim's struggles.* Its near relation is that gem among the flowers, the Sun-dew of our bogs. There is no more beautiful object to a Botanist's eye than this *Drosera rotundifolia*, that puts a garniture of ruby points upon every leaf and has every point tipped with a glittering diamond. In the sunlight it is like some precious jewel. But all this display is death for the unwary insects attracted by this tempting feast. For every diamond point is simply treacherous glue and is to the insect like the mire and quicksand to the higher animals. Every struggle makes his case more hopeless, and he is soon wound in a multitude of threads drawn from those globes of clear waxy dew that distills from the brilliant points and gives

* —but secretes much more to digest him!—Prof. A. GRAY.

the plant its name. When the victim is fairly ensnared the leaf slowly encloses the body, taking days for the operation, and all the slender points bend towards it as though the plant were feeding like the hawk or tiger, on its prey.

Near by this beautiful destroyer may often be found the Pitcher-plant, *Sarracenia purpurea*, of which it may be said, "If the *Drosera* slays its thousands, the *Sarracenia* slays its ten thousands." Where can be found such a death-dealing instrument? one more perfectly fitted for its work? Each leaf forms of its blade a tube or pitcher that becomes a horrid prison. Down deep in its caverns there is a pool of death probably supplied by the plant itself, so that the place of execution is almost ever ready for its victim. The expanding portion of the leaf that serves as a portal to this *Avernus* for insects, is attractive enough and offers no resistance to the various kinds that seek the apparently safe and cool retreat that always stands so invitingly open. The sharp hairs upon its surface all point downwards and gradually lengthen towards the prison. But when the last row is passed there is a steep and smooth passage to that bourne from which so few insects ever return. For if by chance one can drag himself up the steep plane, he is met by those frowning palisades over which he went down with ease, now rising high, thickly set and pointing downward. Those who have gathered these plants in summer and poured out from the hollow leaves the hundreds of decomposing insects, have seen that this machinery has done its appointed work with the certainty of the most cunning beast of prey or the most skilful devices of men.

But all the economy of the plant thus far mentioned probably has relation to its own welfare as an individual. The imitations of Instinct are even more marked in the provisions which the tree makes for its young. In many plants this care extends not only to the maturing of the seeds but in many cases to their distribution.

It is a remarkable fact that in the vegetable kingdom we find the distinction of sex as well marked as among animals—the distinction manifesting itself in some form almost to the lowest types of plant life. If we begin by recognizing the existence of a benevolent Creator, we can readily understand the final cause of sexual distinction among animals, when we estimate the revenue of enjoyment to all higher sentient beings, from the parental relation. But that the distinction of sexes should obtain in the vegetable kingdom where sensation even is unknown, can never be explained on the theory of benevolence in the Creator, unless we look entirely beyond plant life for the objects to be benefited by means of this relation. Such theories might be started in regard to this duality of structure and nature in plants of the same species or double nature of the same plant, as would appear plausible at least to those who are ready to grant that every thing is wisely created for some purpose. But it does not come within the scope of our present subject to propose or defend any peculiar theories of creation. We simply take the plant as it is and trace the structure and function of organs by which the young plants are matured and provided for by their parents.

Among our common plants we shall find abundant illustrations for our purpose ; and the more common the better. When the apple blossom opens in spring, the showy petals, that delight us by their beauty of color and sweet perfume, are but the outer adorning of a much more wonderful workmanship within the flower. In the base of that flower even now, the outlines of seeds can be found covered in the minute ball of tissue destined in time to become the apple. But above those seeds rise the stamens bearing pollen and the pistils to receive the life-giving grains of dust. Lest the work should not be well performed there is honey poured out by the apple blossom as well as by thousands of other flowers, to attract the bees, that in their eager haste to gather the sweet scatter the pollen grains upon the stigmas and distribute them from flower to flower. When the pistil has conducted the substance of these grains of pollen to the seed, it has at once an independent life. It is henceforth a new plant, and the whole energy of the tree is at once taxed to bring that seed to perfection and secure for it the conditions of independent growth. Around the germ, or in some organs connected with it, the tree stores up starch, sugar and other products fitted to support the young plantlet until large enough to gather food for itself from the earth and air. That this provision is for the young plant, is shown by the fact that if the germ is not fertilized by pollen so as to have power of independent growth, the seed fails to fill. This is certainly the rule—if there are any exceptions, they are not more common than parthenogenesis in the animal kingdom. The necessity of fertilization to secure the filling of the seed, is illustrated by what occurs in many of our most useful cultivated plants, especially in the Indian corn. Every silk of the ear is connected with a kernel; and its office is to conduct the life-giving portion of the pollen that may chance to fall upon it to the kernel hidden in the husks beneath. If it does the work, we have the golden rows well filled. But for every thread that fails, a vacant place is found upon the ear in harvest time. The kernel fills with food fitted for the support of the living germ within it. And all that wealth of food for man so abundantly produced each year—the rich harvest of grain that gives stimulus to trade and commerce because so essential to the daily support of animal life, is but the provision which the plants have made for their young.

But when the seed is filled the young plantlet is simply provided with means to start in life—its final welfare depending upon its finding a congenial soil. To secure this, special provision has been made by many plants for the distribution of their seeds. To some seeds balloons of down are fixed by which they are lifted by the winds and scattered broadcast over the land. Others, like those of the Elm and Birch, have a web or circular wing—others still have prongs with barbs that fasten upon men and animals and thus they are distributed by unwilling agents. The *Mistletoe* supplies its seed with a glue that holds it to the branch where alone its parasitic life can be sustained. The student of Botany is amazed at the wealth of invention manifested in this machinery of plants to secure the distribution of the seeds. The plume, the barb, the hook, the spring, the wing in countless modifications are all employed according to the needs of the plant.

But instinct-like provisions made by plants are not always for the benefit of themselves or their young. Plants become protectors as well as supporters, of many of the insect tribe. The Gall-fly has but to deposit its eggs upon the leaf or branch of the Oak, and the tree, like a careful nurse, makes as ample provision for the young insect as is ever made by animals under the guidance of Instinct for their own young. The tree forms a gall or oak-apple which serves as a home and feeder for the immature insect. This provision is not made for one insect alone but for many, and a like provision is made in some form by a multitude of plants. In every case the provision is adapted to the habits of the insect and is always the same in kind for the same species. What is more curious than to see the Oak using its own resources to build a house and furnish food for the insect cast upon its care? The Goldenrod and Potentilla in their swollen stems, the Willow and the Spruce in their false cones oftentimes with an insect under every scale, show in different ways this protecting care of plants towards their insect foes.

LECTURE III.

OPERATIONS IN PHYSIOLOGY SIMULATING INSTINCT; AND THE LOWEST FORMS OF INSTINCT FOR THE WELFARE OF THE INDIVIDUAL ANIMAL SUPPLEMENTING PHYSIOLOGY OR FUNCTION OF ORGANS.

Intelligent and Instinctive Acts.—The Tent-Moth.—Animal Physiology.—Structure, Function and Instinct, supplementing each other.—Unity from system.—Specific Plans.—Servitude of Plants.—Life and its phenomena.—Evolution of the Tree.—The animal body a Machine.—Its Evolution from the Egg.—Variables giving rise to Species.—Alchemists.—Evolution of a specific form, the Robin.—Growth of the bird requiring Instinctive Action.—The first Instinctive Act.—Selection of food.—Relation of Life to the Physical Forces.—Doctrine of Evolution.—Higher manifestation of Instinct in securing food.

WE shall not fail to acknowledge Intelligence wherever we find it. And any act performed because an end is comprehended by the actor as desirable, and because the act is comprehended as a means to secure that end, we regard as an act of Intelligence, whether it is performed by an animal with two feet or four.

But we believe it can be shown that there are many acts performed by sentient beings, that, as means to ends, are the perfection of wisdom, while there is no comprehension on the part of the actor of the end to be reached, or of his act as a means to secure the end. Such acts are truly instinctive according to the substance of the definitions we have quoted ; or better still, according to the popular meaning of the word instinctive. Take for one single illustration, the Tent-moth, that is so injurious to our apple trees. There is not one of them alive in New England this winter month. But probably it would not be difficult to find a bunch of its eggs glued to an apple twig. And when the young leaves begin to expand, a brood of young caterpillars will be ready to feed upon them. They will work together and spin a web or tent for their convenience, making it larger as they need more room. And when their feeding days are over, they will desert the web and each finding a secure place will prepare a cocoon for transformation. All the work of the colony goes on as regularly and with the same certainty in its methods and results as the growing of the leaves, or flowers, or apples upon the tree where it is found. There is no instructor of the young brood, for all the parent moths died the year before. They have no chance to copy. They have impulse and guidance, and do just what it is best for them to do for their own good and to continue the species. They do this without experience and without instruction, and all colonies do exactly the same thing. These are the acts of wisdom and intelligence to which Hamilton refers as being performed while the actors are as ignorant of the end to be accomplished as the water-wheel is of the machinery it sets in motion. To prepare the way for the consideration of these truly instinctive acts, that display a wisdom not found in the actor but which is often ascribed to him simply because the acts are voluntary, we have introduced inorganic nature and plant life, to show that in them we have just such operations as are performed by animals through those acts that are truly instinctive, though often cited as evidence of intelligence and wisdom in the actors. We propose to continue these illustrations of instinct-like operations in plant life and that part of animal life, where volition can have no agency, until we reach that point where the simplest voluntary act is introduced to carry the work of life one step farther than it is possible for it to be carried by structure and function alone. From that point we shall find the instinctive principles of action widening and producing more and more complex results until Intelligence is introduced; and this is introduced chiefly as a means of securing enjoyment, and to carry the being, as in the case of man, into regions entirely above mere physical life, for it is impossible for the mere continuance of physical life to be better cared for than it is by Instinct alone.

In our last lecture we referred especially to those physiological changes within the plant by which it provides for itself to meet the change of seasons, and secure the best condition of growth. In all these physiological functions and adaptations to heat and moisture, darkness and light, we saw adaptation of means to ends such as justified itself to the Reason of man. They all had special reference to the welfare of the individual plant. No careful observer can fail to see adaptation in the parts of a plant working out as specific results as are ever seen accomplished among animals or men. Whatever his theoretical notions of inorganic nature may be, as of something formed and controlled by physical forces working under laws of mathematical exactness, or of species among organic beings as the "survivors of the fittest" in the great struggle for existence, he must recognize among plants an adaptation of parts to produce specific results—results necessary for the existence and well being of the plants themselves as individuals and species. No one pretends that there is any power of perception, any sensation or volition connected with the plant, and yet operations are carried on by it precisely as though sensation, perception and volition were all present.

If we now consider the animal body alone, as far as anatomy and physiology can go, or rather physiology—for that explains the growth—we shall find that it involves the same kind of operations as are in the tree, but more complicated, rapid and marvellous in their results. In connection with all these operations in the animal body there may be sensation, but perception and volition have no more to do directly in building up the animal system than they have in arranging the fibers of the Oak or the angle of its branches with the trunk.

We now wish especially to call attention to the instinct-like operations of vitality in building up individual structures—arranging all their parts and bringing them into harmonious action.

The function of an organ is often what it is, or rather becomes useful to the being on account of the structure of the organ itself or of some part connected with it. Of what use would be the function of the stomach for secreting gastric juice, were the stomach not connected with an apparatus for supplying it with food and also with other organs for the distribution of the nutriment to different parts of the body? What benefit the synovial fluid, if there were no joint to be lubricated by it?

We see structure and function within the animal body producing certain results for the body itself and for the species. In plants, and some of the lowest forms of animals perhaps, the work is completed by these two agencies alone. But when any being is of so high a type that structure and function alone cannot complete the work, then we find Instinct added to act as the handmaid of these two primitive workers, to supply materials or to give a wider range of activities, and finally to bring enjoyment to the individual through its activities. We find Structure, Function, and Instinct in its lowest form, all working together in the same line, apparently for the same purpose, or if for different simple, subordinate purposes, to secure the same complex end. The most careful study of these three agencies in every species only impresses us more fully with the conviction, that they are the three agencies supplementary to each other by which animal life is sustained and has secured to it, its infinite variety of expression. Nothing can well be more unlike than the species that make up the great branches of the animal kingdom. But structure, function and instinct are as perfectly adapted to secure the welfare of individuals belonging to one branch as to another. We may also consider a more complex plan of which these three agencies are but one part. For when we consider the structure, forces and operations of the inorganic world, the structure and function of plants as a whole and the relation of their parts to each other,—the structure, functions, instincts and relations of animals, the plan or system seems to be the same in kind as we see in a single individual or species, but more far-reaching still, embracing as it does the three kingdoms of nature as though they formed an organized whole. But the oneness never impresses us as arising from any likeness of the things among themselves but from the peculiar relationship of the most diverse things to constitute one system, that brings the idea of unity necessarily to every mind that comprehends its parts, relations and operations. Within this one comprehensive plan, by which all beings seem to be related for their mutual good, we may consider the various subordinate plans for specific purposes. These impress us more strongly perhaps because they are specific, especially if they are so different from the general plan as to be unexpected, as the oil gland in the fowl; or if the obvious relation is between two objects having no organic relationship, as the reciprocal effect of animals and plants upon the atmosphere for the mutual benefit of each, or the peculiar structure of many flowers in their relation to the structure of the bee that is to fertilize them. What contrivance of Instinct or Wisdom ever impressed one more than the structure and function of so many Orchid flowers as shown by Darwin, by which the parts are as accurately fitted to the head of the bee as are the parts of a complicated lock to its key? Or who would expect that a plant should have a structure or function, or both combined, for destroying insects? We find these two elements combined in different ways, but each method of operation is as complete for the purpose as any work of Instinct. We are more impressed perhaps, by these specific arrangements for some purpose that has no obvious relation to the good of the being in which it is found. We are not only impressed with the idea of contrivance, but of servitude when we see plants making special provision for their insect foes, providing them at their own expense, with food and shelter.

We cannot help remarking, in passing, that such provisions are an injury to the species in which they occur; and therefore so far as these provisions are concerned, such species exist not through Natural Selection, but in spite of it.

When treating of plants in the last lecture, we spoke of the instinct-like provisions in them as manifested mainly in their outward organs, or in the function of the mature organ. But a like controlling power is manifested in building up every part of the plant, so as to form a complete whole, of complex parts. And of this power we propose now to speak. In the living plant or animal, even of the lowest type, we seem to have an immaterial entity —an essence to which we refer the peculiar characteristics of these organic beings. In the mineral kingdom we find the force of cohesion giving us different forms of crystals from different elements or compounds; but here in the organic kingdom we have *life*, a something which we hardly dare to define, in these days of the conservation and unification of forces—but it is a something that from essentially the same elements, gives us the myriad forms of plants and animals, from the humblest *Algae* to man himself. If we cannot fully understand and define this agency, we can enumerate some of its results. It is from the careful study of these alone that we can hope for more knowledge of the agency itself. *We now see this agency manifested in the production of distinct forms or kinds of beings. For each kind there is also a plan of structure common to all individuals of that kind. Each individual produced by this principle has a cycle of operations that brings the being to individual perfection, then to weakness, then to death, followed by the destruction of the body by chemical agencies. Before death comes in regular order of nature by the completion of the cycle of changes, there is some relationship of that being to the origin of another of the same kind to continue after the first has passed away.* This power then builds up the individual, and from that individual originates another, and so on, giving us the parental relation. In every vegetable and animal this power presides, giving rise to certain activities, which we sometimes call life—or better perhaps, we regard the activities as the evidence that the principle of life is there, and we do this necessarily from our notion of causality. That we do not regard this agency as always active when it is present, is evident in our experiments in the sprouting of seeds. We apply certain conditions to call this agency into action, and not to create the agency itself. The agency once inactive in the germ, under certain conditions, is called into activity and gives a specific result—or rather a long train of results which, from observation on other germs of the same kind, can be predicted beforehand. This train of results consists in building up by evolution, a complicated structure from a single cell of simple structure; in watching over that structure to secure its welfare by adapting its parts and operations to the world, in the same manner as the more general forces of the universe seem to have arranged and prepared the materials of the earth for the introduction of the living principle itself. We can sum up by saying that this force or principle is so far uniform in its operations as to give us the simplest notion of life, which all have, although they may not be able to define it. And this principle that impresses us as *one*, under the name of *life*, manifests itself under hundreds of thousands of the most diverse forms of matter composed of the same elements, and takes for its cycle of operations a single day as in the lower algae, or centuries, as in some of the higher animals. If asked now for the origin of this principle, or of its relationship to the great forces of nature, we are at present, as utterly at a loss to account for them as we are to account for gravitation itself or for the law of its action. We can neither deduce this principle from the analysis, nor synthesis of the forces of the inorganic world. We see that they are conditions for its activity, but this no more shows that it is a modification of them than it follows that because water is the condition of the life of the fish, the fish is therefore a modification of that element. It is a characteristic of this principle in all its manifestations to demand and use as a means of putting forth its activities, the different elements and forces of the inorganic world. If asked for the origin of organized beings we come back in all our investigations where we want something given to begin the work with ; as much so, as we need in Geometry axioms that cannot be demonstrated. When Mr. Huxley has carried us back to PROTOPLASM, we feel that we are as far off from the goal as ever; and although some men stand franticly pointing into the dark, declaring that the chasm between vitality and physical force has been bridged over, we refuse to budge an inch till we see the bridge, and much prefer to be shouted at and even pounded as stubborn, than to follow a logic that does violence to every principle of sound reasoning, both in its assumed data and in its conclusions. And in passing, it is well to remark that there are many points decided authoritatively by scientific men, that common men can judge of as well as they. Because one man knows more of fossil reptiles than another, it does not follow that the latter must accept all the conclusions of the former on every subject. If one does not understand fossil turtles, he may be able to understand a fair argument and to detect bad logic. It has more than once happened that very able and learned comparative anatomists have fancied that they have found the head of an animal where nature placed his tail. But this entire misconception in regard to the structure of an animal, is nothing compared to the arguments that are often accepted because presented by able men,—arguments in which every principle of sound reasoning is reversed, and impassable chasms are bridged over with assertions.

Dismissing for the present further speculations as to the origin and nature of life, since they are only incidental, we will confine ourselves to its phenomena, and especially, for the present, to those phenomena that, like the operations of Instinct, indicate a plan in building up a structure and keeping it in repair, as well as skill in executing the plan. We confine ourselves now to what takes place within the organism by evolution. And we shall find a seeming contrivance and skill shown in the selection and arranging of the materials so that the structure produced indicates a purpose in its several parts and as a whole, and the harmony of the whole is heightened by the function of each part being in accordance with the plan. The perception of this plan is a necessary result when certain relations of the parts are perceived.

Let us now briefly examine the structure of a tree as produced by evolution from the seed. The origin of every tree, as is agreed by all Botanists, is a single cell; or if you prefer to start one step above, it is from a germ, with power of independent life, from the union of cells or their contents. From that minute point starts the Oak with all its complicated and orderly distribution of material. One who has taken the acorn from the parent tree, knows beforehand into just what form the soil around the acorn and the gases in the air will be moulded under the guiding power of the germ which he plants. He knows beforehand what will be the mathematical relation of the leaves to each other, the form and flavor of the acorns which the tree will produce, and he knows that all these parts will be taken from the same soil and air that close at hand are furnishing the materials for a beech, a maple and a pine, perchance.

How inscrutable it is that one portion of that Oak should seek the darkness, plunging down and spreading in every direction where the light cannot come, while another portion as persistently pushes into the sun-light! But after we understand the plan of the tree, we understand that this polarity is necessary for its well being. The presiding power or organizing force had taken care that all parts should be disposed aright to carry out the plan.

How strange, also, that from the subdivision of

one primitive cell, thus forming in the beginning, cells alike so far as we can see, that we should have the proper division of wood and bark and leaves, with their wonderfully complex structure of cells and vessels all arranged for the service of the tree and with power to act so that each should do its part in the complicated machinery of plant growth. But the plan of the tree seems to need all this, and the invisible agency, at the proper time, gives to these cells of common origin the form, position and property, which should make them a fit part of the complex whole. When the proper time comes, the buds all appear in mathematical order upon the limbs, and some of those buds put forth flowers and all the machinery of fruiting, as well as leaves. Look at the thousands of trees and other plants that adorn our fields and forests, and see the plan of each and the skill with which that plan is executed in every outward organ—the plan and execution being the result of that principle within, which secures these varied forms and processes through the agency of matter and the physical forces, as the engineers use power from the same water-wheel and materials from the same store-house, to turn out the diverse products of a varied industry,—cloth and nails and chairs and guns,—according to the design and skill of the workmen in combining the materials for some definite purpose.

We may be told that one part of the plant structure is produced by shortening an axis, and another by the infolding and modification of a leaf, and so on through all the morphology of the plant.

Suppose we grant all this, as we are ready to do, the wonder still remains that the axis was shortened and the leaf infolded and modified exactly as in the operations of Instinct, to produce just the result needed for the welfare of the tree as an individual or member of a species—to say nothing of the original production of the axis and leaf to be so modified.

In the bodies of animals the ministration of this selecting and arranging power as manifested by the function of organs, is of the same kind as seen in plants, but the operations are more rapid, more complicated and wonderful. In the full grown animal we have a machine, and the higher the animal the more diverse the parts and complex the machine. The parts are made of different materials and diverse in form, but all nicely adjusted to each other for a purpose—or for many subordinate purposes, to secure the highest perfection of the individual and the continuance of the species. The body of man or of one of the higher animals impresses us at once as a work of design, but of such design as we see accomplished by Instinct. We can trace the whole process by which the body of any of our higher animals is built up. And we see the same sort of contrivance in the formation of parts, wisdom in selecting materials, and the same sort of skill in manipulating them that we see in the operation of the highest Instinct among bees and birds in the construction of honey-comb and nests. The growing of this machine, after it is once formed with its apparatus all complete, is wonderful enough, but there is something more wonderful, if possible, than the mere growth; it is the original structure of the machine,—the evolution of a complex organism from a mass of matter having no trace of organs,—through the agency of a principle within the matter itself. In the egg of the bird, which is even more complex than the eggs of most other animals, we see a yolk surrounded by the albumen or white. To the eye, unaided by the microscope, there appears one nearly homogeneous semi-fluid body surrounded by another. The microscope reveals but little more—certainly it reveals nothing in the egg that suggests the form or the organs of the bird that is to come from it. The warmth of the mother bird, or an equal amount of warmth from any other source, is all that is needed, and in a certain number of days, varying with the species, there comes from that egg a bird perfect in all its parts. The yolk and white have disappeared. Instead of them you have bone and muscle and feathers, organs of sense and digestion, and the whole complicated machinery of a living animal.

Now within that egg was an artificer that for want of a better name we call *life*. And the process of this artificer's work we can watch from day to day and from hour to hour, if we choose to do so, and trace every step from the segregation of the yolk and faint outline of a living form up to the completion of the work.

But the term *life* is generic, if we consider only

the constant results produced by it. All life does not build up birds any more than all insects build honey-comb. Life has as many specific characters as there are distinct forms of living beings.

We are not now discussing the question how these differences came to be, but simply call attention to their manifestations. We have life a constant quantity, as we should express it in mathematics, and we have joined to this a vast number of variables which give us the forms of life as manifested in distinct kinds. These kinds have not only life in common, but even the variables have something in common, so that the kinds can be arranged into groups according to the similarity of these variables, giving us GENERA, FAMILIES, CLASSES, and finally two kingdoms, animal and vegetable, founded mainly upon the variable, *sensation.*

We do not wish here to be understood as endorsing the view that these variables are constantly changing or liable to change. We only speak of them as variables because they are the cause of differences in forms, all due to one great underlying principle which we call life, which no one fully understands, but the distinctive phenomena of which every intelligent person understands as well as he does the phenomena of gravitation. We regard these variables as the same in kind as those that give rise to the different kinds of matter, or at least strongly analogous to them. We have the generic notion of matter gained from certain properties that must be present to give the notion of matter at all, and then the variables that give the different kinds of matter. The variables in this case are fixed so that probably no man now believes that Sodium and Potassium ever change, one into the other, or Iron into Manganese, or Silver into Gold, though there is great likeness between some of these elements, so great, that some eminent men have believed either that all kinds of matter are modifications of one element, or that each group of elements is a modification of one element. A crude belief of this kind was the foundation of the labors of the old Alchemists. It is certain that the likeness of the elements to each other is such that they can be formed into groups by a truly natural classification as can the kinds in the kingdom of life. The most accurate modern research among the elements, has but satisfied the best minds of their distinctness and that the Alchemists were not only pardonable in being misled by such a mistake but that the mistake itself arose from careful study and great knowledge of the elements which they experimented upon. If those who hold that the variables that make the different kinds in the organic kingdom are of such a nature that we can regard these kinds all as modifications of one original simple form—if those who hold this view should in the end find that their theory is as unfounded as that of the old Alchemists proved to be, we can yet see that this mistake, if mistake it proves to be, has arisen from a most intimate acquaintance with the objects treated of; and we shall be as thankful to them for their great contributions to science directly and indirectly as we are to the Alchemists for the acids and other important agencies and information which they bequeathed to modern chemistry, which certainly would have been far behind its present state had not the transmutation theory kept so many experimenters for ages eagerly at work.

But let us return to the variables in the kingdom of life. In the egg of the Robin, we have not only life but we have in consequence of a fixed variable, if I may be allowed the expression, that particular species of bird. There was life—that could be understood as a distinct thing—and this life was finally to manifest itself fully in the production of the Robin in distinction from some other kind of bird.

Not only are the notions of life, and animal life, and bird life, entirely distinct from the specific notion of the Robin, but they can all be reached by the inspection of the embryo bird by every person capable of comprehension at all, before the specific characters of the Robin would be so marked as to be perceived by the best naturalist in the world who had studied only the adult bird from which the common notion of the word Robin is derived. But the Robin was from the first potentially present in the egg. The materials in the egg do not differ, so far as we can see, either in structure or composition, from the materials in many other eggs; but there is an artificer there such as is found in no other kind of egg. He can build a Robin from the materials and nothing else. This artificer needs a certain degree of heat for his work. The heat may come from the mother bird, from a bird of any other kind, or from a stove. Heat from the same source may call into activity the latent principle in a hundred kinds of eggs at the same time, as the heat from the sun is the condition for the germination and growth of the thousand kinds of seeds that develop into plants every year. It is plain that heat and all the other physical forces have no formative power over organic beings to determine kinds, as these forces exert, or may exert, exactly the same influence over organic beings that in the same place are developing the most diverse forms and properties.

But this artificer in the Robin's egg, being furnished with the proper conditions from the inorganic world, the same exactly as must be furnished in the nests of other kinds for the production of young, selects the materials, joins them together in a certain order, and on a given day presents us with a work as perfect as can be made from the materials in the egg. We have a bird fitted for independent life, and the bird is of a specific kind,—the Robin.

The work now commenced must go on under the same guide or builder while it goes on at all, but the material is all used up. The young bird at once seeks food; if in no other way, by opening its bill to receive it from the mother. It has the appetite arising from the function of its body to impel it to some action, and it is guided in performing the right action without observation or instruction but by a tendency and power of direction that were ready when needed; and for the origin of this power we search in vain in the history of the species. Such a tendency and power are a part of Instinct. This instinctive act of raising the head and opening the bill was needed, and needed at once. Death would come without this simple action on the part of the young bird, in spite of its mother's efforts. It was as needful for the first young bird that ever existed as for one to-day. It is here—it is present in every young bird on the globe that is hatched in so immature state as to be unable to walk.

And here we see the first connection of Instinct with the instinct-like processes below it. There is simply a movement of the head to bring it into relation with something outside of the body. All else is dependent upon the Instinct of the mother bird that supplements this opening of the bill by supplying the young bird with the proper food. And this raising of the head and opening of the bill is no more comprehended by the young bird than he comprehended the distribution of material that forms his head or bill. It is an act performed by all young birds as soon as hatched and therefore can have no relation to experience or instruction. But in the case of those birds like our domestic fowls, that are hatched in a more mature state, the first instinctive act is much more complex. The young bird must select and pick up the first particle of food it ever receives. The very first act of taking food is as complicated in its nature as any subsequent act of feeding can be. This complex act is performed by the bird by the same sort of law as its blood circulates or its feathers grow.

The food gathered either by the young bird or supplied to it by the mother contains the same materials as are found in its own body just formed from the egg, because Instinct guides in its selection. Physiological function of the mother supplied the egg from which the body of the young bird was formed, and now her Instinct leads her to supply, through volition, her young with additional substance of the same kind. The Instinct of the young bird and that of the mother both join to bring more material within the working sphere of the same artificer that first formed the bird from the materials in the egg. But how unlike in appearance from the substance of the egg, are the grain and insects now supplied to carry on the work! But Instinct recognized them as proper materials before chemistry was known, and from these materials, that inscrutable something that formed the bird within the egg now carries on its work to completion. It enlarges bone and muscle and feather. This is growth, which at first sight seems a simple matter compared with the evolution of a perfect bird with all its complex tissues and system of vessels from a single cell, but in reality it is just as difficult of comprehension, or rather just as far beyond our comprehension as the other. The materials used we understand perfectly, and the process of digestion and distribution we are able to trace very fully. We see in the process the action of chemical affinity and mechanical forces; but while all this knowledge is a great gain to us it is not all. We no more feel that we know it all now than we did before Chemistry and Physiology were studied. We see chemical action and mechanical structure and osmose just as far as our best glasses will carry us,—but we see certain results which we cannot find in these agencies any tendency even to produce, except as they are servants to prepare and distribute materials. The organizing force itself and its wise action in building up the organism are no nearer our comprehension than they were before Spencer and Huxley wrote. Growth in a complex being requires selection of material in proper kind and quantity to be carried to certain places, and there to be molded into certain forms for a certain purpose, in a self-acting machine having power of rapid and complex adjustments to the constantly varying conditions of the inorganic world and all organized beings with which it comes into any relation. It is not enough that Lime and Iron and Silica are carried to certain places, but they are selected in proper quantities and carried where they are needed for a specific purpose; and there they are mingled with other materials according to the office they are to perform, and then are molded into bone and feather, beak or talon, as the case requires, according to the leading idea of the machine in which the work is done. All this is entirely different from the work of Chemistry or Mechanics,—so very different that we see no more tendency in Chemistry and Mechanics to set this machine in motion and preside over its operations, even with the aid of all the favoring conditions of the universe, than we do in a finely adjusted machine to start itself. The origination of organized beings through the direct agency of physical forces and perpetual motion, seem to us to stand on the same plane scientifically considered. But if one doubts this or can see farther and discern a transmutation of forces unperceived by common minds, still the fact remains that there is something within the living body that works with a purpose in regard to the whole structure at any given time, for its preservation and also for the continuance of the kind. It not only selects proper materials for its work, but it stores up material for use at certain times, as fat in the fall of the year for the use of hibernating animals, and lime in crustaceans to suddenly form the new shell when the old one is cast. It thickens the covering for winter and throws off hair and fur when they are no longer needed. When bones are broken or wounds formed, it sets in motion machinery to repair the damage. In all this we see going on within the body perpetually the same sort of work that we find going on out of the body through that agency which we call Instinct. And however diverse these bodies are in structure and the function of their organs, we find the Instinct connected with each, fitted to carry out to perfection the work begun within the body where the senses and volition of the animal have no agency in the operations. We can say of every animal that we find its Physiology and Instinct working together, one always supplementing the other so far as Instinct is needed to secure the life of a single animal or the continuance of the kind.

And so far as we can see, the structure, function

and lowest form of Instinct by which the animal takes food, propagates its species and cares for its young till they are able to care for themselves,—all these must have been present from the beginning of each species as it now exists. If present species have been derived from other species, then Structure, Function and Instinct, must have moved on in every change in the individuals that survived, so as to be properly called the ancestors of the present species.

It is only fair to remark that this is no argument against evolution of species from one form, if we suppose this evolution provided for in the beginning and all these activities arranged to come into play at the same time and work together, as the parts of a clock are so arranged by its maker that the hand shall point to the figures and the hammer give the corresponding number of blows—or as all the organs of a flower are so arranged as to act their part at the proper time for the fertilization of the seed.

Having made these general statements in regard to the connection between the instinct-like operations of physiology and Instinct itself, we may enlarge more upon the method in which Instinct takes the first step in securing the welfare of the individual. We have already referred to the Instinct of the young bird which enables the mother to provide for it. The peculiar Instincts of the young we shall refer to in another connection. We speak now of the adult in his simplest act for the preservation of his own existence. The selection of food is the simplest instinctive act that has relation to the whole complex organism, and it is the lowest that involves any exercise of the senses as a condition for the exercise of the Instinct. This selection of the proper kind of food may come to be essentially connected in the adult with very complex activities and animal powers of a high rank.

In the lowest forms of *entozoa* there seems to be no volition in taking food, so far as we can see, even in the adult. The food is simply absorbed. The coral polyp also is stationary, as is the oyster, and both must feed upon materials brought to them by the waters, though very likely there is volition exercised by both animals in the process of selecting materials from the waters. But the most wonderful part of these animals, that which evinces the most evident design—the coral cells that form the coral branch or dome, and the pearly shell—are the simple products of growth,—volition neither originates nor changes them. In higher animals we find Instinct manifested not only in selecting food from materials presented, but in seeking for it and securing it. To do this, it is sometimes necessary that the Instinct of one animal shall take advantage of or circumvent the Instinct of another. The Bald eagle takes advantage of the Instinct and labor of the Fish-hawk to procure fish for himself by robbery. The Arctic Jager obtains its food by persecuting the Gulls. And a Southern Gull steals from the Pelican. The cat tribe know without instruction how to watch for prey. Those animals that must feed in winter when no food can be obtained know how to gather in stores, though they may never have seen a winter. Those that sleep in winter, simply prepare a nest. In both cases, Instinct supplements function. Migration from place to place, as the supply of food changes, is the method of solving the same question for many birds. Function thickens the coat of the animal for winter. This provision is just as needful as any thing Instinct can do, but Instinct is not burdened with any thing that function can perform. All that relates to providing food in the first instance is left to Instinct. That action of the system by which it lives upon the fat stored up in the fall and the change that takes place in hibernation by which the expenditure of material is lessened, are certainly functional changes. These are instinct-like provisions of the system; but the securing of the food in the first instance was done by a principle that supplements structure and function; and this principle is something entirely different from them, and something that no structure or function of the animal system would suggest the existence of, except as we have learned by observation that there always is in the animal a directing power which we call Instinct, to supplement the structure and function of organs and thus to complete the work commenced in the body.

LECTURE IV.

HIGHER FORMS OF INSTINCT FOR THE WELFARE OF THE INDIVIDUAL OR THE SPECIES, HAVING NO IMMEDIATE RELATION TO STRUCTURE OR FUNCTION OF ORGANS.

Intelligence guided by experience.—Instinct inaependent.—A natural development.—Building of nests or homes.—Perfection of nest no test of the animal's rank.—The facts of Building stated.—Relation of Building to Structure and Function.—Variation in Building.—Swallows.—Thrushes.—Oriole.—Black-birds.—Sparrows.—Nests from different localities.—Mr. Wallace's Theory.—Difference in Building Power.—Improvement by Practice.—The Cow-bird.—Supplementary Instinct of the Foster-parent. Change of Instinct compared with change in plants.

IS that Instinct or Reason? is the common question, when an animal performs some act that commends itself to the Reason of man. Where we find animals adapting means to ends, the conclusion is often reached that there is Intelligence to guide the act, when the very wisdom of the act proves it to be instinctive,—that is, an act performed without any comprehension by the actor of the end to be reached. Pure Instinct works out the wisest results with the certainty almost of the operations of the physical forces of nature. And because these results are wise, in the sense of being adapted to secure the welfare of the actor, and because volition is brought into play, it is a very natural thing to refer such acts to Intelligence in the actor, which adapts means to ends through a comprehension of both ends and means. Great confusion has arisen from a failure to understand that the first introduction of Intelligence, while it widens the sphere of action, always renders wise results less certain in the beginning than they are in the sphere of pure Instinct. Instinct can be cheated, as we shall show, at the proper; time but it is only in the sphere of Intelligence that mistakes and blunders are the common result, until experience whips the being of Intelligence into the right road. Pure Instinct needs no experience. It goes before to preserve life until knowledge from experience is possible. And in this work of preserving life where experience could not be secured, it often performs wise acts,—just such acts as in beings of Intelligence are performed only after individual experience or instruction from the experience of others. We must throw aside at once then that notion that an act of wisdom and intelligence is absolute proof that the wisdom and intelligence reside in the actor. That question can only be determined by considering the conditions under which the act is performed. The best corrective to these hasty conclusions that have been formed respecting the nature of Instinct in animals, from the kind of acts it secures, is found in the careful study of those operations performed by plants; because in them, there is no danger of being misled so as to ascribe wisdom to the actor. This is one reason why we have pointed out so many of these peculiar processes in the vegetable kingdom. The same instinct-like processes were traced in the evolution of animals, that we might find the exact point where Instinct comes in to carry on the work which the structure and function of organs both demand. We cited as the simplest instance of Instinct, the act of the young bird just from the shell, that lifts its head and opens its bill to receive the food needful to carry on the work thus far carried on by the use of the material in the egg. The material in the egg was just sufficient in quantity and had the proper proportion of elements to form the bird. The young bird came from the shell with a structure capable of receiving food, with an appetite to demand it and with an Instinct to receive it from the mother as in the case of the Robin, or to select and secure it for itself as in the case of the young of the domestic fowls.

And these three agencies, Structure, Function and Instinct, were all ready to enter upon their joint action at the same time. And the nature or complexity of the Instinct varies with the complexity of structure so as to exactly supplement it. If this were not so the animal must die. So the wonders of Instinct are no greater than the wonders of physiology in preparing and distributing food for the building up of the system, or the wonders of the eye that is ready for seeing without any knowledge of optics on the part of its possessor. Instinct, pure and distinct, in all its complexity, is as natural a development according to fixed law, as wings or teeth or claws according to the wants of the animal,—and the origin and development of one is just as far beyond our comprehension as the other.

The taking of food is a prime necessity for every animal. The necessity begins almost at the instant independent life begins. It returns with regularity or at least with absolute certainty so long as the vital functions continue their normal activity. And any failure to meet the demands of the appetite for food and drink prevents all development and ordinarily brings speedy death.

The necessity for building nests or homes has no such immediate relation to the organization of the animal. And in the work of building we are introduced at once to the higher and more complex acts of Instinct.

In the case of many animals, the building is simply a contrivance for rearing young; the home never being used except for the production and care of the young, and therefore not being any thing growing out of the constant necessities of the individual, as is the taking of food. Some animals never build at all, either for themselves or their young, as is the case with most fishes as well as with many of the larger quadrupeds; and even some birds lay their eggs upon the bare rocks or grass. There are examples enough from all departments of the animal kingdom, in different parts of the scale of rank, to show that building is by no means a prime necessity even for the care of young. And it is further to be remarked that the skill in building is by no means in proportion to the rank of the animal in the intelligence of its acts in regard to other things. In fact those animals which in their structure and mental qualities seem to approach nearest humanity, either build in a very rude manner or not at all. In many cases the skill to build seems to be greater as the animal is lower in the scale. Certain it is, that the nest is no test of the capability of the animal in any other direction. It seems to be something which the animal has the impulse to build and the skill to build because it needs it for its own welfare or that of the species, as the silk worm winds the cocoon for a tomb in which to pass to a higher condition of life.

There are certain things in reference to this tendency to build and the skill in doing the work that are not only curious but may have an important bearing upon the theories respecting the origin and development of animals.

1. We find in some cases the building material wholly or partially secreted from the body of the builder,—as the silk with which the different species of spiders weave their webs or form their curious nests, and the wax for the Honey-bee's comb. In the case of many other animals the sizing or cement is apparently furnished from the body of the builder, as in the case of hornets and wasps of various kinds that make paper and the hardest kind of paste-board of woody fiber. The American Swift or Chimney-Swallow, also glues together the sticks to form its nest with a cement from the glands of its throat.

2. Among animals very nearly allied there is

great diversity of building as is seen especially among bees of different kinds; as the Honey-bee with its waxen wonder and the Bumble-bee with her few uncouth cells, chiefly the deserted cocoons of her brood. The Carpenter-bee and others give still more diverse methods. Among the wasp tribe we find those that build with woody fiber and others that build with clay. And both of these materials are wrought into varied forms by different species of the wasp tribe.

3. The building is sometimes the work of the male alone, as in the case of the Sticklebacks among fishes; and sometimes of the female alone, as the nest of the Paper-wasp prepared for the first brood of workers in the spring; and sometimes it is the joint labor of both male and female, as among most birds.

And then in other cases, all the care of building belongs to a set of workers that never produce young themselves but seem to have their whole energy concentrated on the work of providing for and defending the young of others. The White-ants and Honey-bees are the best examples of such builders.

4. Those animals that show the greatest range of building power are those that build in the rudest manner; and those animals that attract the greatest attention by their complicated and skilfuly constructed homes, are those that work almost with the exactness of machinery.

5. When we find different methods of building practised by the same animal, we generally observe the same uniformity in carrying out each of these methods, as we find among animals having only one method.

The house of the Muskrat, built of mud and reeds in shallow waters, and the burrow of the same animal where he can find steep banks, are two methods by which he adapts himself to the different conditions of the places he inhabits; but each method is as uniform, in itself considered, as though that were the only method practised by the animal.

In a certain sense, the structure of an animal's organs and the functions of his body have a relation to the home he prepares, for it is by structure alone or structure and function combined that he is enabled to build at all. But the impulse to build in the large majority of cases is one that has so remote a relation to the structure of the animal or his wants, and his ability to build so far transcends what we should expect from an examination of his structure, that we could never tell beforehand how any animal would build. Nothing can well be more unlike than the homes of animals that we should naturally expect would build in the same manner.

We see no tendency in the function of producing young even to originate the impulse to build or to give the skill to build the numerous kinds of nests found in the animal kingdom. In some cases we see the need of the nests and dens if the young are to come to maturity at all with any degree of certainty; but the need arising from certain conditions does not in any manner account for the origin of the impulse to do a given thing, or the marvellous skill often manifested to meet the conditions which the necessity imposes.

If we consider the nests of birds for instance, which are the animal homes best known to us, they nearly all are made simply for the care of the young; but no one could tell from the examination of a bird, what materials it would select for its nest, its method of combining them or the position of the nest. Birds very nearly allied differ much in their habits of nesting, and yet in each case the nest is so uniform in its structure and surroundings as to be in general characteristic of the species. That is, birds of the same species, under the same circumstances, build with like materials and in like positions. Any departure from the common method of building in any given locality will be found, on careful examination, to be very slight, and to be so uniform in the variation, according to the surrounding conditions, as to appear to be a manifestation of a wider range of Instinct than had generally been attributed to the bird, rather than a result of intelligent contrivance, as is seen among men. The variation in the form of nest once seen can be described as the certain work of the animal when circumstances demand or favor the change; the new manifestation of instinctive knowledge and skill being made in a specific method to meet the new conditions.

We need only call attention to a few of our well

known birds to show that each species instinctively gathers the same materials for its nests, combines them in the same manner, and selects for its nests similar positions; and also to show that birds of the same family, and even of the same genus, differ more from each other in all these particulars, than many birds do that are far removed from each other, according to the structure of organs and apparent ability to build.

One of the Swallow family, like a skilful mason, fastens its nest of mortar against the frame-work of the old barn; another, with the same materials, fashions a more curious nest still, beneath the eaves of the same building,—both species preferring these places, when they can be found, to such places as they are compelled to select beyond the habitations of man. Another Swallow makes her grassy bed in a hollow tree, another digs deep holes in steep sandy banks, for its young. The so called Chimney-swallow finds its favorite home in hollow trees or in the chimney of the farm-house, where it plasters its hard nest of sticks against the mason work with a cement secreted from its own body. If we class this bird near the Night-hawks, as some do, the difference in nesting is as marked, for the Night-hawks can hardly be said to form nests at all. No examination of these birds would enable the best Ornithologist in the world to predict what materials would be used for the nest of each, the form of the nest, or its position. The facts can be learned by observation only. But when the habits of each species, in nesting, have once been learned, they are always given in describing the bird as something so constant from generation to generation,as to be worthy of study as characteristics of the species.

Among the Thrushes, the well known Robin builds its rude nest of mud and grass in almost any elevated place, while other birds of the same genus, as the Brown thrush, use no mud in the construction of their nests and often place them upon the ground. The brilliantly colored Oriole weaves her pendant nest upon slender, drooping branches. The nearly allied Crow-blackbird builds its nest entirely unlike this, of coarse materials, on the most solid basis it can select, while the Cow-blackbird, like the European Cuckoo, never builds at all; but deposits its eggs in the nests of other birds that its young may be cared for by them.

Most of our sparrows build simple nests upon the ground, while the Chipping-sparrow, like the Canada Bunting, is known as "Tree-sparrow," and also as "Hair-bird," because it generally builds in trees and lines its nest with hair. What can be more curious, or mark more strongly the peculiar nature of Instinct, than that thousands of birds of the same kind should form nests of the same pattern, selecting materials of the same kind for the different parts, when no possible reason can be given why another form would not do as well for the bird and be as easy for her to build!

It is true, when we examine nests of the same species in different localities, that we find difference in material, difference in the perfection of the work, and difference in the position of the nests. But when we have discounted all these differences, there remains a permanence of type to the work of Instinct in each species, almost equal to the permanence of structure, size, color and other characteristics that mark the species. So that we may fairly say that the uniformity of Instinct in the work of building, approaches the uniformity of physical function in giving character to the animal.

We have here then two very distinct statements to make that seem borne out by careful observation.

First,—That in the same species there is in general great uniformity in all the elements of building, as to materials, form, skilful work and position. And,

Second,—That birds so nearly allied as to belong to the same family, and even the same genus, build in such diverse methods that their nests have little or nothing in common, except that they are nests.

If we start with the assumption that each family of birds came from one ancestor, it is perplexing to understand how the slight differences of structure which mark the distinction between many species, should be accompanied by such change of Instinct that there should be such great diversity in building among birds of nearly allied species inhabiting the same district; and yet such great uniformity and permanence of method among birds of the same species.

That the Baltimore Oriole should always hang

its nest as it does, or that the Chipping-sparrow should line its nest with hair, and so on of the peculiar characteristics of the nests of hundreds of birds, are things which cannot be satisfactorily accounted for, by any appeal to the force of habit or any thing connected with the physical nature of the bird.

It has been noticed by Mr. Wallace, in his valuable contribution to Natural History,* that birds generally build with the materials most convenient for them; and this is undoubtedly true as a general proposition, as it is true that they eat the food most convenient for them. And they select for their breeding-places regions where the conditions of building and feeding are best for them. This selection of localities by long journeys even, is a part of their instinctive work.

But it is not true that birds select the most convenient material for building to any such extent as to lead us to infer that they learned to build with any particular materials simply because they were abundant. For different kinds of birds living in the same region, build their nests upon very different plans, and very many of them build of materials that are by no means abundant. It is difficult to tell why the Great-crested Fly-catcher uses the cast-off skins of snakes in building its nests; but, certainly, it is not because they are the most abundant materials that it can find.

If the exact material the birds wish for cannot be found, they select that most like it as a substi-

* "Natural Selection," p. 215.

tute. The materials are then woven in a manner peculiar to each species, so that the nest of the bird, in very many cases, can be as certainly known when found deserted as it would be with the bird upon it. And when a new bird is discovered and its nest is found, that is described with nearly the same expectation on the part of the Naturalist that all other birds of that species will nest in the same manner, as that they will produce eggs of the same size, form and color. The character of the nest depends not only upon the material used but upon the form and the method in which the material is combined. The theory is broached by Wallace,* that the young bird studies the nest, and so builds by imitation. To say nothing of the want of observation which he shows in talking of the young birds as coming back to the nest, which seldom, if ever, happens among birds that build open nests, as the large majority of birds do,—he seems to overlook the fact that skill in combining the materials for the nest, is the marvel. It is not so much that the bird knows *how* the nest is made as that she is able to make the nest at all,—especially that certain kinds of birds are able to build such complicated nests the first time the attempt is made. Let Mr. Wallace study the nest of a Baltimore Oriole or of a Chipping-sparrow twice as long as the young birds remain in it, even counting the days before their eyes are open, and let him then go to work with all the implements the most skilful mechanic

* "Natural Selection," pp. 222–3.

can furnish,—let him work a month, and if he can produce as good a nest as the bird will build in a week with its beak and claws, we will listen patiently to the arguments to prove that birds learn by observation to build nests. We can hardly do so now.

But it is said that some nests of the same species are better built than others. Certainly. Sometimes undoubtedly it is impossible for the bird to find the best materials; sometimes there may be structural difficulties in the bird that interfere with skilful work, and it would certainly be different from any thing else in nature if we did not find birds of the same species differing somewhat in the nest-building power, as they do in size, beauty of plumage and power of song. It is possible that there is real improvement by practice, as Wilson long ago suggested, but there are no facts that are conclusive proof of it. And after discounting all differences found among nests of the same species, we have still remaining in the manufacture of some nests, manifestations of skill that no human workman can approach with the same materials. A careful examination of the nests of birds will convince any one that there is given to each species, without experience or instruction, a tendency to build nests, that arises as spontaneously as hunger arises at stated times from waste of tissue. There is also an impulse to select certain materials for the different parts of the nest; and this impulse is as fixed as is the law of growth which gives to the bird a certain color or thickness of feather, both of which may vary according to the different conditions of the bird. And lastly, there is the skill to combine the materials; and this comes by the same sort of law as that by which the talons of the bird of prey are fitted for their work, or ornaments of color and form of feather are so skilfully arranged on birds as to challenge the admiration of the greatest masters of art. The perfect form of beak and talon and the ornamentation of feathers are the result of growth; but because the work of building nests involves *volition*, the same sort of wisdom and skill are often referred to the bird as would be found in a human being who could perform the same work. But a human being having Intelligence, that is, the power of comprehending the relation of means to ends, would be compelled to study and work long to gain the knowledge and skill which the bird has as an original gift—as it has fine feathers without borrowing them and artistic ornaments without labor or price. Intelligence, wherever found, has the blessed privilege of laboring in order to learn, and the condition of enjoyment through learning, never ends; but the knowledge and skill of Instinct come without effort. There is no joy in acquiring and no basis for self-improvement from Instinct alone. The animal doomed to live under the guidance of Instinct alone, has its knowledge and skill at the appointed time as regularly and as spontaneously as hunger or thirst.

That birds may have a ray of Intelligence we shall not here pretend to deny. When we come to trace out the relation of instinctive acts to the work of Intelligence, we may be ready to grant to some of them a good measure of Intelligence. What we wish now especially to controvert, is the doctrine that all Instinct is the result of observation, either of the present races or of past races, from which the fixed habits have been transmitted, or that high wisdom and skill manifested in an act, are any certain proof of comprehension on the part of the actor.

One of the most conclusive arguments against this doctrine, that birds build nests by observation or the study of the nest in which they were hatched, is found in the habits of the Cow-bird (*Molothrus pecoris*) already referred to. This bird never builds a nest at all. The young Cow-birds wake to life in all sorts of nests where their mothers deposit their eggs,—in Ground-sparrows' and Tree-sparrows' nests—in Warblers' and Vireos' nests. Now according to the observation theory, we ought to find these birds building nests; and such nests as each one was raised in. But we find Instinct asserting its sway. In the spring time we see hundreds of these birds in New England congregating together—not with the birds in whose nests they were hatched. We find them with a note of their own and in spite of their opportunity of observation and in spite of the care of their foster-parents, we see these perverse birds refusing to build nests of any kind, but putting out their own young to be cared for by other birds, just as their own parents did. They follow the habits of their parents, *although they never saw them*, and perversely throw aside all the instruction of their foster-parents, which they enjoyed oftentimes to the detriment or destruction of the rightful birdlings of the nest.

We here observe two things that impress us with the blindness as well as certainty with which Instinct operates, when performing those works which often appear so wise. The Cow-bird simply finds a nest, deposits an egg and leaves it to its fate. The Instinct of the mother stops there; and the whole race of Cow-birds would speedily become extinct if this apparently defective Instinct were not supplemented by the Instinct of the foster-mother that broods upon the egg as though it were her own, and then feeds the strange bird hatched from it, until it becomes twice her own size, it may be, and entirely unlike her own young. Though this young intruder often pitches all the rightful occupants of the nest upon the ground to die, yet the foster-mother does not generally detect the imposition practised upon her. If her Instinct were not at fault there would soon be an end of Cow-birds. But if Cow-birds are to exist at all, then the perfection and wisdom manifested in the foster-mother's Instinct consists in the certainty of her being deceived and thus doing for the Cow-bird the work which its parent refused or failed to do for it.

In a certain sense the nest-building Instinct of birds is connected with the function of producing young; but the connection is very remote compared with the connection between hunger or thirst and the Instinct that enables the animal to satisfy the appetites. At the proper time the bird returns, it may be from the south, to its proper breeding-place, chooses its mate, if that were not done before the journey commenced, and in due time commences the work of nest building. The peculiar nature of Instinct is shown first in this, that the bird builds its nest before it is really needed, and also in the materials selected, their skilful arrangement and in the form and position of the nest; all constant or very nearly so, in the same species.

All the differences that have been pointed out in nests of the same species of birds are not greater *than can be pointed out in the habits of the same species of plants, by which, through some law of their growth, they adapt themselves to the conditions of the place where they chance to grow.* We are prepared to say then that while we do not deny a degree of Intelligence, even to birds, we regard their most perfect and wonderful works, those often referred to as proofs of Intelligence, to be the products of Instinct that works by a wisdom of which its possessor has no comprehension.

LECTURE V.

SOME MANIFESTATIONS OF HIGHER INSTINCT.—RELATION OF INSTINCT TO SPECIAL STRUCTURE AND FUNCTION.

Relation of the Appetites to the Instincts.—Perfection of the work no proof of Intelligence in the Actor.—Test of Intelligence.—Flexibility of Instinct.—The Ampelopsis.—The Bean.—The Potato.—The Knowledge of Enemies among Fowls.—Common defence.—Simulation of death.—Instinct and Climatic change.—The Musk-rat.—The Partridge.—Instincts learned from observation alone.—Instincts essential to life.—Origin of instinctive powers.—Hibernation.—Difficulties of the Natural Selection Theory.—Special Structures.—The Rattle-snake, Bee, Wasp and Hornet.—Relation of Instinct to color and form.—Cases cited from Wallace.—Relation of Instinct to Experience.—Seventeen-year Locusts.

We have thus far treated of Instinct chiefly as supplementing structure and function of organs, either directly or indirectly. There is a certain function of the stomach that produces the sensation of hunger. Instinct takes up the work and allays this craving by supplying the materials that satisfy it,—and the materials that satisfy it in each animal are the materials fitted to prolong his life and build up the body. This chain of means is complete. The links all join together—they are links of physical necessity, if the animal kingdom is to be kept on this globe. In hundreds of kinds of animals they are as ready to do their appointed work the instant the animal bursts from the egg, as they are at any subsequent period of life, as in the case of the majority of insects and fishes that never know a parent's care.

It is sometimes said that hunger is instinctive. A careful consideration of the activities will show this statement to be an abuse of terms. Much confusion has arisen by confounding the appetites with the Instincts or from a misapprehension of their relations to each other. The appetites proper, as the appetite for food, arise directly from the functional action of some organ. The functional action of the stomach, for instance, producing hunger, calls Instinct into play to procure the proper food. And this may be said of the appetites, that they are the condition for the activity of certain Instincts calling them into play to carry out to completion the work, to which the appetites furnish the first impulse; that is, the continuance of the individual or species. Some of the works that have their origin in an impulse of appetite are so complicated that they give rise to whole series of acts involving a varied and wonderful adaptation of means to ends, as is the case among birds in all their work of rearing young referred to in the last lecture. *But so long as the same results are reached by the same means by thousands of individuals without experience or instruction, we have no ground for inferring that there is comprehension of means and ends in the actor.* In fact the more complex and perfect the work performed, *provided it is performed without instruction or chance for experience,* the more certain it is that such work was blindly performed under the control of some law of life, as certain in its action, and yet as free from wisdom or contrivance in the actor, as the growth of organs or the activity of the organs when the good of the being demands it. Intelligence in the actor works by no such uniform methods.

But it is said there is not only adaptation of means to ends among animals but such a variation of action according to the change of conditions as to show comprehension on the part of the actor. If there is truly comprehension and specific action in consequence of it, showing that means and ends and their relation to each other are all understood by the actor, then we plainly have intelligence. But in many cases there is no proof of comprehension where it is claimed. It seems to be the nature of Instinct to vary within certain limits to meet the change of conditions in the world around it, as the balance-wheel of the watch, made of different metals, adjusts itself to almost continual change of temperature so as to give uniform results in the movement of the watch. It is the office of Instinct to do a certain work to keep the animal in the world. To do this it must vary somewhat in its action according to external conditions, but no more, nor in a more wonderful manner, than the organs or functions vary in their activity in both animals and plants, to meet the change of conditions in the world around them. Does not the eye adjust itself without Intelligence, to the change of light within certain limits? Does not the coat of fur thicken upon animals as winter approaches, to be thrown off again, without volition, when the warmth of spring makes it no longer needful, but a burden? Even among plants, we find such change of action according to surrounding conditions, that nothing would save them from being charged with acting by contrivance and forethought, except that they are plants. If a Woodbine (*Ampelopsis quinquefolia*) can find a support on which it can wind its tendrils, it will do so, like the Grape-vine and many other climbing plants; but if it can find no such support, it will fasten the ends of its tendrils against the smooth walls by broad disks and thus hold itself in place. This beautiful vine was evidently made to climb walls; and within certain limits, its method of growth changes to meet the circumstances of the case. A bean, which must climb, hunts for a pole by causing the terminal bud to describe larger circles as the vine lengthens. It will find the pole on one side of the hill as well as on the other within certain limits,—that is, if the pole is near enough for the vine to reach it before its weight brings it to the ground. It will, even then, often make a second attempt from its new centre of support. The eyes or buds of the potato may be pointed towards the centre of the earth, but when the sprouts start they will bend and, avoiding all obstacles that oppose them within certain limits, will push their way to the light. These and a multitude of other plants not only show adaptation of means to ends in their mode of growth, but the mode of growth varies according to the conditions in which the plant is placed. In the animal kingdom there are just as plain cases of variation of method where no comprehension can be fairly inferred, but where it is often presumed to be present simply because the acts are voluntary. We have here another illustration of the value of a more careful study of plant life and the functional changes of the animal kingdom to adapt its members to the conditions, of the world, in correcting many hasty conclusions and in leading us to study the conditions of any act more carefully than is generally done, before we refer its wisdom or the contrivance manifested by it, to the comprehension of the actor.

We have perhaps sufficiently considered the Instincts as ministering to the demands of the appetites. But there are instinctive acts that have no possible relation to the appetites or any function of organs, so far as we can see. They arise from some power of knowing, or mode of acting, given to the animal as its original endowment, such as could be gained by man only from experience or instruction. The fear of a particular enemy is an example, as the fear of birds of prey by our domestic fowls. Fear of danger is an Instinct common to all animals as well as man; and a bird may certainly learn by experience, that certain things are dangerous. In all cases where an animal learns by experience, there may be a claim set up that there is Intelligence; though here there is great need of caution, as many cases of apparent learning from experience can be fairly brought under that principle of Instinct, which we have already explained, by which it varies within certain limits, to meet change of condition in the world around it.

But the peculiar fear which all grain-eating birds have of hawks, even when they are seen for the first time, is marvellous. The domestic fowls always know their enemy,—raise the cry of alarm,—and even the young chickens rush to cover. Young birds of other kinds, in the nest, unable to fly and as yet having no experience of evil, shrink with wild terror from a hawk.

The fact that the fowl knows every bird of prey at first sight, as something to be specially dreaded, is a thing that marks the manifestation of Instinct as peculiar; and for the existence of this peculiar terror no rational account can be given, except that this instinctive dread is an original endowment of the fowl, without which the species would be destroyed. All attempts to resolve it into habit or experience, seem to us to utterly fail, as we shall attempt to show in a future lecture. It is one of the original outfits essential for the preservation of the species, and therefore could no more be left to experience than the Instinct for selecting food could be left to experience.

There is not only instinctive recognition, by the fowl, of the hawk as an enemy, but Instinct also makes every fowl a sentinel for all the rest of the flock. The first one that sees the enemy does not seek its own safety alone, but instantly raises the cry of alarm, which all its fellows, even the youngest, instantly understand. That note is like no other, but it is common to all fowls when the enemy is seen. This peculiar fear, the note of warning, the instant recognition of it by all others, and the impulse to hide when the alarm is sounded, are, taken together, a perfect adaptation of means to ends; such as might be arranged among men by agreement. But here we find this social machinery in operation at once among all fowls. Each one acts its part instinctively, with the same precision and certainty as its hunger comes to aid in the preservation of its life, or its wings grow in the best mechanical form for flying.

Among grain-eating and insect-eating birds there is also a common call or warning note, heeded not by one species only but by many, when there is common danger from birds of prey. It is not an uncommon thing to see hawks chased by several kinds of birds at the same time, especially the sparrow hawks, that are dangerous to the small birds. A most remarkable instance of this united action of the different species of birds in protecting each other, came under my own observation. A small owl was fastened near a house in daytime, and was accidentally seen by a robin, that raised the alarm of danger. Instantly, from all directions, the note was answered, and birds of different kinds were seen flying towards the spot. Within five minutes, more than fifty birds, representing fourteen different species, were in the tree and doing what they could to drive away or torment their common enemy, the owl.

There are other methods of saving life by instinctive acts, that are so uniform and yet vary so much in details to suit particular cases, that they are worthy of study, as parts of that complex machinery by which nature provides for her species, so that they may have a fair chance in the struggle for existence.

The simulating of death is a common instinctive act with many animals. If we referred this device to any comprehension of means to ends by the actor, it would, in its different manifestations, be ranked with the most adroit cunning among men. But the varied conditions under which this instinctive act is manifested, forbid our referring it to any thing but an original gift, as free from contrivance on the part of the actor as is his form or color. The simulation of death is common to many of the insect tribe and to the Opossum, whose success in the trick is so well known as to make his name a byword. We find the same simulation of death among the young of some species of mice, so long as they are helpless, while the Instinct seems to be lost when they are old enough to care for themselves in other ways. Before their eyes are open, they will go through all the contortions of dying animals, and finally put on the perfect semblance of death. When we consider the low rank of the Opossum, the most successful counterfeiter of death among adult vertebrates, and also that this device is most common among insects, and is also found among the helpless young of some animals, we shall see that this apparent cunning and contrivance are simply capabilities given to compensate for the want of other powers, and that they are the result of spontaneous impulse, saving the animal, he knows not how.

There are many instinctive powers ascribed to animals the existence of which is not certainly established—as the power of perceiving the change of weather. Some animals may possess this power as an Instinct, but there is need of more observation on the point, before it can be accepted as established. Undoubtedly they are influenced by climatic change, as men are, and many of them probably to a much greater degree; but a careful examination may show that many acts now referred to Instinct,are simply the result of physical exhilaration or depression, through climatic influence, and that these are therefore reflex, rather than instinctive, acts. Certain it is, that Instinct is not a perfect guide in reference to climatic change; for many animals perish every year because heat or cold, or moisture or drought, are more severe than their Instinct had provided for. Under the impulse of the Instinct of migration, birds often come north in spring to perish by storms of snow and cold, which would not happen if Instinct were the perfect weather prophet which it sometimes has the credit of being.

It is supposed by some, that the severity of the coming winter can be predicted from the character of the walls of the houses which the Muskrats build. After carefully observing the work of these animals for more than twenty-five years, and comparing the predictions with the results, I cannot believe that the Muskrat knows any thing, beforehand, of the severity of the winter or the height of the coming freshets. He certainly makes serious blunders. He sometimes builds his house where the water leaves it in winter and the frost renders it useless. And, again, he builds it where the freshets overflow it and compel him to shift for himself among the ice and water. The Muskrat provides for winter as many other animals do, but the uncertainty of the season is a condition which seems to be an important element that he has to contend with in his struggle for existence. The thickness of the walls of his house, according to which the severity of winters is predicted, seems to depend upon the condition of the weather while the house is building, rather than upon any foresight of its builder as to the coming winter. As the Muskrat cannot control the height of the water, as does his cousin the Beaver, he is often compelled to add to his house as the water rises and then again as it retreats, while he makes his canals and approaches deeper. He is often kept at work upon his house till winter closes in. What affects one lodge is likely to affect all more or less, in the same region; and thus in meeting the exigencies of the case, from day to day, these animals have had credit for a foresight which they do not possess.

The safety of all species is that their Instinct provides for the average season,—our protection against many animals, that is, against their too abundant increase, is that their Instinct fails to make provision against the extremes of seasons. When certain insects become abundant, it often happens that a single season rids us of the pest because their Instinct fails to meet the exigency of the case.

The common Partridge, or Ruffed Grouse of our forests, knows how to protect itself from severe winter weather by plunging beneath the light snow. Its Instinct leads it to take advantage of the non-conducting power of the snow to sleep in warmth and comfort, while the storm is raging above. This act is beautiful in its relation to the welfare of the bird, and shows that Instinct is here wiser in its action than the Intelligence of some men, who perish from cold when they might protect themselves perfectly with a covering of snow. But while the Instinct of the Partridge teaches her to protect herself from the storm by plunging beneath the snow, it does not teach her that the falling snow may turn to rain and be succeeded by cold; which sometimes happens, so that the poor bird is imprisoned by the hard crust, to die of hunger or be dug out by some prowling fox that thus finds a Partridge ready trapped for him. It is not uncommon to find the evidence of such mistakes of Instinct, or want of instinctive foresight, in our New England forests late in winter. The Instinct of the bird which leads her to seek protection in the snow, is upon the whole, good. It contributes to the comfort and safety of the species, while it sometimes works injury to the individual bird. This is another example of the great law of nature, that there shall be a constant struggle for existence—that no individual of any species, can be perfectly protected against accidents and early death; and that Instinct itself, which is sometimes called "unerring," may be the means of destroying its possessor, by the very agencies which it calls into play to preserve him.

The power of some animals to find their homes when carried from them under such conditions that they cannot observe, and even to take a straight course towards them, is generally acknowledged. It is contended by some that the Carrier Pigeon is guided by sight, while others deny it. While we believe some animals have this instinctive power, it is difficult to determine the facts in the case by observation. And if established, they would be only one more illustration of the principle already considered, that animals have, as an original gift, all those powers needed for their mode of life.

The many points in regard to which we are still in doubt respecting the habits of our most common animals, show that we still have need of Hubers and Wilsons to study every species. Not only do our story books, but our school books, abound in statements that nature refuses to endorse. And learned writers often trust to such unreliable statements, or ignore the facts that contradict some favorite definition or theory. Fortunately for our purpose, there are examples enough to illustrate every point we wish to make, that are repeated from year to year, so that they can be studied by every careful observer.

In the manifestations of Instinct last considered we see evident relation to the welfare of the individual or the species to which it belongs. These Instinctive powers give such ability to act as experience might be supposed to give; but the ability being needed before it could be gained from experience, it appears as part of that outfit with which the animal is sent into the world. But the principles of action in many of these cases, are of such a nature that there is nothing in the organization of the animal to suggest their existence. We learn of their existence only by observation. There is nothing in the structure of birds to indicate to us with any certainty where they will build, or the form of their nests. We know that the fowl gives the cry of danger at the sight of the hawk, and that its young seek cover at the alarm, because we have seen the frightened brood thus guided by Instinct. We readily see the wisdom of the thing, but it is impossible to learn from the structure of the animal that it will perform these particular acts, as we could infer from the talon and beak of a new species of hawk that it would live on flesh, or from the structure of the web-foot that its possessor would seek the water.

Instincts that minister directly to the appetites, are common to all animals as an absolute necessity to them. They must act promptly, or individuals must perish, until the species disappears.

Instincts that protect animals from their most fatal enemies are common to many species, ready to spring into action the instant the enemy is perceived, even for the first time. And such an Instinct seems to be almost as essential to the preservation of some species, as are the Instincts that minister to the appetites.

It may not be out of place to refer in this connection, to the bearing of some of the facts thus far considered on the origin of these powers which animals possess, as well as upon the origin of the species themselves.

If we adopt the theory of transmitted skill gained through the experience of previous generations, which has much that is plausible in its favor, we are forced to the conclusion that there have been ancestors of our wild animals of very great ingenuity in devising and executing plans, and that these ingenious beings have appeared in great numbers among the insects; and we are also troubled to see how the species, in many cases, continued upon the earth till these ingenious beings appeared whose wisdom and contrivance, inherited by their descendants, seem now absolutely essential for the continuance of the species from one generation to another—in many cases, for their continuance for a single year.

If we appeal to Natural Selection, as is now frequently done, we have indeed a powerful agency to work with; but will it do the work we need to have done? Natural Selection, granting all that is claimed by those who invoke its aid for the solution of all problems in regard to the habits and structure that characterize species of animals,—Natural Selection is simply "*the preserving of the fittest.*" It does not give a characteristic to any animal, but simply preserves him through the agency of some characteristic which he already possesses. Natural Selection does not give to the animal the power to hibernate, for instance; but the most it can do, is to preserve those animals that already have this power in the greatest perfection. But in the conditions of hibernation we find an exceedingly complicated machinery for the preservation of animal life, varying much according to the species. There is a chain of agencies of which Instinct is only one link. Hibernating animals of the higher rank, feed upon food that is abundant in the autumn. Their appetite is then voracious, and fat accumulates to an unwonted degree. So far, Instinct has no part in the work except in the procuring of food. But now it comes in as chief actor, to impel and guide the animal in preparing a nest or retreat for his winter's sleep. When this is done, function takes up the entire work again, lessens the rate of breathing and lowers the whole vital activity, so that the animal lives for months without eating, and yet comes out in good condition when nature has once more spread a table for him. In the case of other animals, especially in the case of some reptiles and insects, there is complete torpor. But in every case we see these agencies, Instinct and Function, working together, or rather working in succession, each supplementing the other.

It may be said that cold has a tendency to lower vitality, and so by degrees these functional changes are produced and the animal, or more strictly the species, forms a habit which we call Instinct. But if we go to certain hot countries where great heat and drought are combined, we find animals secreting themselves by Instinct and becoming torpid in summer, as they do with us in winter. The exact counterpart of hibernation is there repeated under entirely different conditions. Instinct is as perfect in its work there as here. Its object in both countries is to aid in saving the animal when his food fails and the extremes of climate are too severe for him. It does its work well; but it would utterly fail in both hot and cold countries, if the functions of the animals did not supplement it in producing those remarkable changes in vital activity, rendering multitudes of animals here torpid in winter, and there in summer. Instinct has not only to meet these different conditions, but it must vary in both places, in many ways, to meet the wants of different species of animals. And in this whole work of hibernation,—if it be proper to apply this term to the change that occurs in hot countries,—in all this work of hibernation, which is a wonder in itself, we find Instinct true to its character as thus far traced, as an agency spontaneous in its action supplementing the physiological agencies, to preserve the individual and species.

If now we claim that all these hibernating animals are what they are because Natural Selection has been going on from age to age until only those are left that Structure, Function and Instinct all combining, have adapted to the conditions of the world in the northern regions and under the equator, the question still returns, How were the species preserved till these changes in action were all brought into harmony with each other and with the world without—until adaptations were secured that singly or in a long series, seem now essential to the very existence of the species?

Another question also arises; how were the changes which have resulted in these complex adaptations inaugurated? If we refer all these results to accidental changes accumulating in the right direction, we confess it would be as easy for us to believe that the words of a book might be formed in order by a series of accidental positions of type thrown from a box. If we refer any of these nice adjustments to the comprehension and contrivance of animals in the first instance, then we are called upon to recognize in the ancestors of the present races a power of comprehension which these races do not now possess—a comprehension equalling that power in the best of the human species; for no man can claim that he could better adjust these activities of the animal with the forces of the inorganic world, than they are now adjusted. And these adjustments were complete as they now are before men could understand the work even.

And it must constantly be borne in mind that to explain these results through the agency of Natural Selection, we must see how it could secure not only all the difference of Instinct that there is in the world, by the accumulation of changes all working out a specific result, and the difference of form and internal structure by like accumulated changes; but we must see how it can secure *all of these at the same time*, so as to produce the specific forms in their wonderful variety and the specific instincts in their complexity, and yet bring structure, function and Instinct to harmonize in every one of the hundreds of thousands of species,—and each individual, through these combined agencies, into the best relations with the world in which it lives.

In addition to this, before we can accept Natural Selection as the chief agency in the production of species, we must see how all the species were kept in existence while those slow changes were taking place which now give the species character and upon which their existence seems to depend. The explanations of the best masters, after giving them the benefit of every fact they present, leave many, perplexing difficulties, in regard to such relationships as we have already referred to. The problem will become more difficult as we advance. Some of its difficulties are well illustrated by the examples under the next topic,—

The Relation of Instinct to special structure and function.

If we accept Natural Selection as the means of securing the special adaptations of instincts and instruments which we see among animals, we must grant that in every case, there was at the beginning, an instrument and an instinct to use it effectively; because an instrument without the corresponding instinct would be of no advantage to the animal, but a damage. Where we find special structures or special functions and corresponding instincts, we must grant the co-existence of both and the conjoined action of both, before Natural Selection could possibly have any influence to preserve either of them in the species, or the species themselves through their action.

Without attempting, at this point, to discuss the questions that might arise as to the origin of the conjoined structure, function and Instinct, we proceed to call attention to a few facts that illustrate the subject, and at least show more fully than has thus far been done, the diversity of action of the instinctive principle, and also how Instinct supplements structure and function of organs, in higher planes of action than the mere securing of food.

We take as our first illustration that dreaded reptile the Rattle-snake. We here find, first, the grooved or perforated fang,—its point sharpened like a chisel, on the most approved principles. This instrument is folded away when not in use, but unsheathed and in position the instant it is needed. As the tooth grew, all the straps and springs needful for its most effective use grew with it. At its base grows a gland secreting a deadly poison; and the opening of that gland is through the hollow tooth. When the tooth makes its wound, the same motion that drives it home, injects the poison. The whole machinery is perfect. Structure and function both agree in a complicated but perfect manner. The result of their combined action, is death to the victim. Now comes in the third element which we call Instinct, guiding the voluntary action of the snake. The tooth and the poison would have no terror for us, were it not that the snake will strike and do it effectively without instruction!

But the rattle of this reptile is another peculiar

contrivance related to its Instinct. The rattle gives a note of warning to animals. It is of no apparent use to the snake, as it ought to be according to the Natural Selection theory; but, on the other hand, it is likely to bring death to its possessor by giving notice to its enemies of his presence. If the rattle is beneficial to the snake, it appears when least needed, for when the snake is young and most likely to be injured by its enemies, it has no rattle. The rattles grow as the fangs grow, that make him dangerous to other animals and to man. We find this instrument of warning and the Instinct to use it given to this snake that, on account of its great numbers and wide distribution, would be exceedingly dangerous without them.

In this reptile then we have the perforated tooth with all its complicated adjustments, the deadly poison to accompany it, the rattle to give warning as he becomes dangerous to other animals, and an Instinct to bring into effective action all these special structures and functions.

In the Bee and Wasp and Hornet, we have the instrument for defence, the poisonous secretion and the Instinct to render them effective. But in the Honey-bee, we have much more than these provisions for defence. Its Instinct leads it to store honey for use in winter. We pass now the complicated but special apparatus that enables the Bee to gather the honey, to consider the conditions that enable her to store it. After being gorged with honey, she secretes scales of wax under the rings of the body. This substance, essential to the economy of the bee-hive, is not produced by any work of Instinct but by a peculiar function of the body. Those scales of wax the Bee softens, undoubtedly, by another peculiar secretion; and then fashions them into a cell that has challenged the admiration of the world.

Let us trace this process through. There is an Instinct for gathering honey and, answering to it, an instrument just fitted for drawing it up from the nectaries of flowers. There is also a sack for holding it and for producing certain changes in it. There is an Instinct for storing this honey and a substance secreted that can be molded into cells to hold it. There are instruments given for using the substance to the best possible advantage, and Instinct to guide in the best use of both instruments and the substance. Instinct comes in at the proper place to link all these agencies together. Let a single link be wanting and all other parts of the chain are useless as a means of preserving the species. And complicated as this whole process is, it is only a part of the connected series of functional and instinctive adjustments absolutely essential to Honey-bee life, as the species now exists.

Among the Wasps and Hornets that build nests and cells of woody fibre, we might trace out the relation of Instinct to structure and function, showing results almost as curious as those already considered. In fact, instances almost without number can be given in every department of the animal kingdom where structure and function, either separately or combined, are joined with an Instinct that gives them their whole value in securing the welfare of their possessor.

Among spiders we find, perhaps, the best illustrations of the great diversity of the results produced by the joint action of these three agencies, in animals very nearly allied. A whole lecture might be given in showing the varied uses to which different species of spiders put this web-making secretion which is common to nearly the whole spider tribe. We have webs of a multitude of forms—fine threads, as treacherous snares—curious nests lined with satin, and homes beneath the water; besides sacks and covers, from the thinness of gauze to the thickness of paper, to protect their eggs and young. The problem does not seem to be; In how few ways can Instinct avail itself of function to provide for the family of spiders? but rather, In how great a multiplicity of methods?—as though diversity were the object aimed at; and yet each method would challenge our admiration, if all spiders in the world were found using that alone.

In this connection we cannot fail to notice the relation of Instinct to form and color.

It is well known that many wild animals correspond in color very closely to the coloring of the earth and herbage where they live. Among the higher animals, especially among birds, every careful observer has noticed that many of them seek those places where their colors will best harmonize with the surrounding objects. The Grouse, already referred to, so closely resembles in color the withered leaves among which she places her nest, that the keenest eye seldom discovers her. Though one of the wildest of birds, she settles herself upon the nest and seems to trust in the deceiving power of her feathers, and so remains quiet until the foot of the intruder is almost upon her.

The Ptarmigan Grouse of Greenland and the Sage-hen of our Rocky Mountains are both beautiful examples of what the united action of color and Instinct can do to protect the bird. I have frequently seen both of these birds light, and yet have been entirely unable to distinguish them from the surrounding vegetation until some movement of the bird aided the eye. There is also change of color from summer to winter and the instincts of the animal are in harmony with these changes for its welfare.

But it is among insects that this correllation between form and color and Instinct, is most readily observed and most wonderful. There are insects that simulate leaves so closely that they deceive careful observers. Mr. Wallace gives an interesting account* of insects that imitate, in their structure and color, decaying and diseased leaves. And Instinct here aids in the work of deception; for these insects fasten themselves upon limbs in such places and in such positions as withered leaves would naturally be found in. A spider† is also found, according to the same author, that resembles a bud in appearance, and his natural place of concealment is

* "Natural Selection," pp. 59–61. † Ib. p. 99.

in the axil of a leaf, just where a bud would be found.

But every observer of our own insects has seen among them examples of this correllation of Instinct with form and color. Some of our caterpillars have the color and form of short sticks. They, in case of danger, fasten themselves upon a limb and extend the body so that men and birds are both deceived; so completely do color, form and position mimic a dry stub upon the bush. The curious thing is, no matter now how it has been secured, that Instinct should come in among butterflies, spiders, caterpillars and hosts of other animals to complete the work of deception, which is begun by color and form, simulating the common appearance of leaves in all their changes and flowers and buds and sticks.

In every step that we have taken in this investigation, we have found Instinct becoming a part of a more complex system of agencies, but still filling a place which function of organs alone could not possibly fill—securing results that might be obtained through experience and instruction by some animals if there were any way to provide for the continuance of the race of animals until experience could be gained. But in the case of those animals that could possibly learn by experience, something must go before it. There must be impulse and so much of guidance as to preserve the animal till experience can come to his rescue. But with many animals knowledge from experience is impossible, because there is occasion for performing the most important acts only once in a lifetime, and that too under such conditions as to make it impossible that the actors should learn from others. In such cases we find Instinct ever ready to do its work—a work sometimes so complex as to require careful study on the part of man to understand it. This point can perhaps be made plain by a single illustration. The *Cicada* or Seventeen-year Locust is so called because it appears only once in seventeen years. The insects deposit their eggs in the limbs of trees and die. The young grubs find their way to the earth and there mine in the dark for seventeen years, when they come forth for their few days of life in the sunlight. When they come out they are to deposit their eggs and do all the work which their ancestors did seventeen years before. They do the work but once in a lifetime, but every movement goes on in perfect order, as though experience and instruction both had done their perfect work on beings capable of comprehension. They copy exactly the work done by their ancestors seventeen years before, when they themselves existed only in the eggs.

We have thus far found Instinct as meeting the demands of appetite—as protecting its possessor from special enemies, and as taking its place, with color and form and function, as a higher agency for preserving the life of the individual and the species. We have found nothing yet to indicate that it is an entity, a thing by itself, as it is often represented to be,—a possession which animals have in common.

It seems rather to consist of a summation of spontaneous activities which animals possess in different measure and of different kinds, according to the sphere they are to occupy.

LECTURE VI.

INSTINCT FOR COMMUNITIES OF ANIMALS.—ITS RELATION TO THE DOCTRINE OF NATURAL SELECTION.

Illustrations of the Community System.—The Cow-bird.—Three kinds belonging to the same species.—Necessity for slaves among Ants.—The brood or annual flock.—Permanent organization.—Leaders.—Sentinels.—Pelicans of Utah Lake.—The Beaver.—Morgan's Work.—The Rank of the Beaver.—The Muskrat.—Variation of Instinct necessary.—Complexity of work no proof of Intelligence.—Consideration of theories.—Accumulated work of Intelligence.—Instinct like it, in effect.—The Honey-bee.—Bumble-bees and Wasps.—Slave-Ants.—Darwin's Explanation.—Difficulties.—Natural Selection and Variation not sufficient.—Wallace on Natural Selection applied to man.

IN almost every manifestation of Instinct thus far introduced, the act has been one for the preservation of the individual or species, but such as the individual could perform for itself. A single pair at most, caring for their young, in all their instinctive acts would represent not only so many individuals but the species as a whole.

We began, however, to see the introduction of another principle, when we found adults uniting in action to aid each other; one species of birds even calling to their aid others, of different species, against a common enemy. And when we found a system of instinctive acts, by which alarm-notes are sounded by birds for the benefit of their fellows, and safety thus secured to the flock, we began to see the community system, which prevails extensively in the animal kingdom and gives rise to very distinct and complex manifestations of Instinct.

When the community system becomes prominent, a single animal, or a single pair, often becomes a very imperfect representative of the species, if we wish to study the whole work of Instinct. Individuality is lost in the machinery of the community. And so far does this system prevail among some species, that a single male and female cannot possibly care for their young. In more than one case the species could not possibly exist without the aid of individuals from other species. In such cases, the dependent species have an Instinct to secure the services of other laborers and thus supplement their own defects.

In the case of the Cow-bird, already referred to, the species would perish were it not for the work of other birds in hatching and feeding the young Cow-bird. But so far as we can judge, this defective care of the Cow-bird for her offspring arises entirely from the action of its Instinct,—defective action when taken by itself, but effective when we consider its relation to the Instinct of other birds whose work it secures. We see nothing in the organization of the bird to prevent it from nesting and rearing its brood like other birds. But lower in the scale of being, we find three kinds of animals belonging to the same species—the males, females and neuters—all needful for carrying on the work of life. And in some communities of Ants, the in dividuals of another species are needed to make the system perfect. That is, the first species could not exist at all were it not that their Instinct enables them to supplement their own defects by making slaves of individuals from other species able to do their work for them. We announced in the beginning of these lectures that we should make no attempt to collect and rehearse the wonders of Instinct. Our object is to bring up for consideration those examples of instinctive action known to every Naturalist, or such as all persons may see if they choose to. We are therefore compelled to refer briefly to points that might be illustrated by many examples.

There are among animals certain instincts that either grow out of the relation of the sexes or are indirectly connected with it. Thus we have the flock or brood for a single season, or so long as the young need the parents' care. This Instinct is an entirely different thing from that which prevails in the community proper, which ministers to the good both of the individual and of the species, not through any relation of the sexes or of parents to their young necessarily, but by the organization of a complex community of adults that may have no relationship to each other except that they belong to the same species. The simplest form of such communities is found among common birds and beasts that associate in flocks. These, as Sheep, Antelopes, Crows and Pigeons, might do very well as individuals; and a single pair can, not only, care for their young without aid from others, but at the time of rearing young, the flock is generally broken up, each pair caring for its own. It is after the breeding season is over and the young are able to shift for themselves, that flocks and herds are formed among many of the social birds and beasts. This may, in some cases, be done simply from love of society. Here the work of Instinct seems to be simply to increase enjoyment. But in very many cases, perhaps ultimately in all, there is a certain organization of the flock; and that organization is made in some way subservient to the welfare of the individuals, as such. The most simple case of united action, is in following a leader. There seems to be, in flocks of animals of various kinds, some individual that leads either in migration or in defence. This leader is generally the most powerful male of the flock. But another advantage to the individual, from the flock organization, is seen in the selection of sentinels, that are posted to give warning, while the others feed. Among common fowls, each one is ready to give warning of danger; but among many wild animals there is often coöperation according to a system, and a very excellent system too. Crows and Pigeons may be seen watching upon the trees, while their fellows feed in the meadow. At the approach of danger, these sentinels raise the alarm which is the signal understood by every one of their mates. Those that watch in the beginning, are from time to time relieved, while others mount guard in their places. It is impossible to tell how it is arranged, that the distribution of labor shall be just; but a careful watching of the flocks, shows that there is a regular system for change of sentinels.

Major Stansbury* gives us an account of the young Pelicans at Utah Lake being watched over by one old Pelican, while the others were engaged in fishing. Each sentinel or guard, was regularly relieved, in turn, by another taking her place. Here the community system was introduced among these birds for the purpose of caring for their young. But as he found one old Pelican, though blind and unable to fish for himself, still sleek and apparently well cared for by his fellows, it is fair to infer that the community system, among these birds, secures to some extent, mutual aid among adults.

I have myself seen something of this community of action, in the care of young, among the Arctic Tern on the coast of Greenland. One little grassy island, that I had the opportunity of watching for eight days, was entirely occupied by Tern. They made no nests, but deposited their eggs among the grass. The island fairly swarmed with their young, from those just out of the shell to those of full size, ready to fly. The old birds made common cause against any intruder; and it was settled by observation, that they did not always feed their own young. Three different adults were seen feeding the same young bird that had been placed upon a rock by himself. All the young seemed to be well cared for; but how the favors of the old birds were

* Ex. Doc., No. 3 Senate, Sp. Sess. 1851.

properly distributed, among such a scrambling multitude of young, is a mystery.

As a farther illustration of the advantage to the individual, from the community, we have animals that build together and enter upon extensive works for the common good. The Beaver is generally considered as the best example of animals of this kind, —at least among the vertebrates. There is hardly an animal on the globe that offers more curious instinctive habits for study; and hardly one that has been more misrepresented in our popular works. The wonderful instincts of the Beaver, make up an interesting part of those story books where fact and fiction are mingled together; though the facts, if fully stated, would be more wonderful than any fiction.

The world is indebted to Mr. Lewis H. Morgan, of New York, for a work on the Beaver, that is a model for all to study, who would investigate the habits of any animal. He has swept away a mass of rubbish that we used to be taught; and has substituted in its place the plain facts gathered by years of personal observation among Beaver-dams and lodges. He not only describes what he has seen, but he brings before us copies of Beavers' works, by photographing them as they are found.

His facts are reliable—his speculations based upon those facts may, of course, be accepted or rejected by any one, according to his estimate of the proof presented to establish each point.

Mr. Morgan grants that the Beaver is a social animal, but he denies that Beavers work as organized colonies, as it has generally been supposed they do. He seems to think that they work as families; but that each family is quite distinct in all its works from every other family around the pond. He supposes that a Beaver-dam is generally begun by a single pair, and that it grows by the labors of all the Beavers inhabiting the pond in after years; but that each Beaver works by himself, in making the additions or repairs, except where a great injury calls many to work at the same time. Then they do not come as an organization under leaders, but each does the best he can. He certainly makes out a very clear case of the community system, so far as the inmates of a single lodge are concerned;—and the impression is left on some minds that there is something like concerted action on the part of all the families, inhabiting a pond, for the preservation of the dam. Certain it is, that members of each lodge do their part of the work, whether they do it in concert with the others or not; and they do it in such a manner that the result is the same as that of organized action. We find dams, and lodges, and burrows for escape. There is a straight entrance to the lodge for the introducing of wood, and an abrupt entrance with winding channels, for the escape of the occupants, in case of danger. There is the cutting of timber, sometimes of trees two feet in diameter. Wood is stored up beneath the waters for winter food; but how it is kept under the water, no one can yet tell with certainty. The refuse wood, after the bark is removed, is preserved for repairing the lodges and dams. In fact, the whole social economy of a Beaver colony, is as perfect as though they worked by an organization like that of the hive-bee; and the facts as detailed by Mr. Morgan, are certainly as wonderful as any fictitious story of Beaver sagacity ever printed. When we read the book we wish that every animal had such a historian; that we might know something more of this world of ours than we do, and have reliable materials when we wish to investigate any question respecting the habits of the beings around us.

But when our author begins to speculate in regard to the mental powers of the Beaver, we feel called upon to dissent from many of his conclusions, while accepting the facts that he uses, as established.

After acknowledging that the Beaver stands very low in his physical organization, he ranks him very high in Intelligence, on account of the complexity of his works and their adaptation to his wants. And by intelligence here is meant simply the power in the actor, of comprehending means as securing an end desirable and good for himself, in all his relations; in distinction from that voluntary action that secures the same kind of good for the actor, where comprehension on his part, is plainly out of the question. The same course of reasoning, by which the power of comprehension is ascribed to the Beaver, on account of the complexity of his works and their adaptation to his wants, would place the Honey-bee high in the scale of free intelligence. There is, indeed, more variation in the work of the Beaver to meet different conditions of life, than the Honey-bee is called upon to exhibit. But the uniformity, with which Beavers do their work in any given place, and their uniform change of method under different conditions, seem to point to that variation of the instinctive principle, to which we have already referred, rather than to free intelligence,—a variation no greater than is found even in the growth of plants, to adapt them to different conditions of life, but which, because in animals it is connected with volition, is very likely to be regarded as a sufficient proof of comprehension in the actor.

The Muskrat, which is nearly allied to the Beaver, has the same sort of variation in his habits to meet the conditions where he is placed. But the variation is so uniform that the animal is plainly under some guiding power which is to him a law of action. Muskrats, whose ancestors have for generations burrowed in the banks of the stream, will at once begin to build houses, if a dam is raised so that they can no longer burrow. And those houses will be built like all other Muskrat houses, the world over. That is, there will be that generic likeness which shows that the lodge is built under the impulse and guidance of some principle entirely different from the power of comprehension and contrivance, seen among men. Since it is impossible that all animals of the same species should find places exactly alike to build in, the impulse and guidance, which for a better name we call Instinct, would be folly itself, if it did not vary sufficiently to meet the conditions of the case, under all ordinary circumstances. Therefore on the theory that Beavers are guided by an Instinct that directs without intelligent comprehension, on their part, of means and ends, it is not strange that their houses grow thicker and larger as they grow older; and that repairs and changes are made as the number of occupants increase. The uniformity in the character of their work, under similar conditions, is certainly in favor of the theory of guidance by Instinct. And the very complexity of the works, upon which Mr. Morgan bases his argument for the high rank of the beaver in free, self-conscious Intelligence, we regard as an argument against it, because we have complexity with such uniformity. In proving Intelligence to be the controlling agency in contriving and carrying out all these complex works, he seems to prove too much. For if we refer all the works of the Beaver to Intelligence, of the same kind as man possesses, we must concede to him abilities very nearly, if not quite equal to those of man, for planning such works. For he would be a wise man that, having only the Beaver's instruments to work with, could do his work. In fact all his works, that we do understand, we approve of as the best that could be done, even by us, to reach the same ends; and he does some things that the wisest man does not yet know how to do. There is complexity and uniformity under similar conditions, —variation in the work of the whole species when the circumstances demand it, and yet under all these conditions, a uniform method of adapting means to ends in the best manner. If all this comes from Intelligence in the actor, he is certainly of high rank.

Among all the animals thus far mentioned, the community might be considered an entirely accidental thing; though in this case, the organization of the community, manifested in the appointment of sentinels and the notes of alarm, must be considered the complicated mechanism of Instinct in many, working together for the good of the individuals composing the community; or, if the organization be regarded as the outgrowth of experience and the result of contrivance to meet the exigencies of the community, we must be ready to concede to all these animals as well as to the Beaver, a high degree of Intelligence and the power of adapting means to ends as perfectly as is ever done among men for such purposes; and we must also grant them high powers of generalization and induction and as plain principles of prudence, as men ordinarily manifest. Nor does it change the question to say that this provision made by flocks is now mechanical, but the result of habits acquired gradually long ago under conditions of danger and need. If there is found among any species of social animals an organization by which, as a community, they are provided for or guarded against danger by sentinels and signals, which can be referred to their Intelligence at all, as a system marked out by them from the comprehension and adoption of a plan, then that plan was worked out by the flock which we see before us, or it was worked out by some individual of that flock and impressed upon the others by a system of instruction, or it was worked out at some time,by some ancestors of the present flock, and continued till it became a habit of the whole species to operate according to this plan. A thing must be done for the first time before it can become a habit; and it must be often repeated, before it can become a habit for the individual even; and much longer before the habit could become hereditary, if at all. So that the doctrine that Instinct is formed through the influence of the experiences and habits of ancestors, only removes the difficulty one step farther back. Nor does it change the matter to say that the result we now see is the effect of minute changes brought about through great cycles. Each change was a step, and when the process was complete through many steps, it represented the same powers in the *species* as though the steps had been taken in a generation. A cotton-mill is the result of great experience continued through many generations of men; and it also represents the contrivance of hosts of men in the present and past ages to meet the wants which experience suggested. But the cotton-mill to day, is as truly a product of human thought, as though the present generation had built one now for the first time. And the first machine invented showed the same kind of power in the inventor as the last and most complicated. So we say that these manifestations of Instinct among social animals, taken as a whole, or divided into the greatest number of steps possible, must be the result of impulse and guidance given to animals just as we now see them manifested, or they show the same high powers in kind, in the animal, as the man possesses who studies them and approves of them as the perfection of wisdom for the individual animal and the flock.

But we now come to consider certain social animals that cannot exist, except as communities. There is, in some species, such difference in structure and function and Instinct in individuals of the same communities, that there is a division of labor marked out and made necessary by the very nature of these individuals. The peculiarities found in some species that make the organization of the community most efficient, are destructive to isolated individual life.

Of such animals, the Honey-bee is a good example and the best known. We have in this species, the Queen-mother, the drones or males, and the workers; in the latter of which there is no power of reproduction. Without the Queen-mother there could be no continuance of the species, as she alone produces all the eggs for the swarming hive. The Queen and the drone, it would seem, would alone be sufficient to secure the continuance of the species. But not so; for they do not even collect honey for themselves, to say nothing of their numerous progeny. To complete the organization of the hive, there must be another class, the workers, which shall collect food and do all the work of building for themselves, the Queen and young. The conditions for an organized community are now complete. The great mass of individuals in the hive, gain their reputation for industry by working for the common good,—for Queen and drone and young,—as well as for themselves. And to this complicated organization, the instincts of each individual are adjusted, so that each performs its part, as each organ of the body performs its office, or each official would perform his part in a perfectly organized kingdom.

Among Bumble-bees and Wasps we find different kinds of individuals in the same community as in the Honey-bee hive, but these communities continue only a single season. The fertile females alone survive the rigors of winter, while the multitude die and the old nests are deserted never again to be inhabited. These mothers, that are to preserve the species, hide away in secure resting-places, till spring calls them forth to commence alone the founding of new colonies.

Different species of the common Ant, as well as the so called White Ant, afford marked illustrations of this diversity of structure, function and Instinct in members of the same species, for the good of the community.

It has been known since the time of Huber the younger, that some species of Ants make slaves of the neuters of other species. The Red Ants of Europe (*Formica rufescens*) not only make slaves of the Brown Ants (*Formica fusca*), but are entirely dependent upon them, being utterly unable to take care of themselves. We here see a need so imperative that this whole species of Ants would die in a single year without the Instinct of making slaves; and what would their slaves be worth if they had not the Instinct to do the work? And yet they are always fresh importations and, being neuters, have no power to reproduce their kind and transmit the habit of being a slave, as an Instinct.

Darwin has acknowledged all these facts in his work on the origin of species.* With his accustomed thoroughness, he set himself to verify the statements of other Entomologists by his own observations. After satisfying himself of the facts, he goes resolutely at work to make this state of things appear consistent with his theory; though he confesses that at first it seemed fatal to it. After a careful examination of his arguments to show that all these differences might have been secured by Natural Selection, we are compelled to say that not only does he seem to fail in fairly meeting the objections that he himself acknowledges to lie against his theory, in these phenomena of social insects, but many more objections and more perplexing, must arise in the mind of every naturalist who has so far studied the facts in the case, as to be able to fairly bring them to the test of Mr. Darwin's theory; or rather to test the theory by them.

Mr. Darwin thinks the wonderful Instinct of the Honey-bee, by which it builds cells that he acknowledges could not be improved upon, might be accounted for in this way.† The making of wax takes a great deal of honey; and so it would come

* "Origin of Species," 5th Am. Ed., pp. 225–232.

† Ibid., pp. 223, 224.

to pass that those swarms of bees which build with the least wax, would have most honey left for winter, and so be most likely to live. The best builders would in this way, be preserved, while all the poor builders would, in time, die off.

Here it will be observed that the theory does not go back far enough to account for the whole case. At most, it simply offers an explanation of the preservation of those swarms made up of the best builders. But we want to know *how the bee became a builder at all?* and how the Instinct to build cells and the function of secreting wax fitted for the work, began together; and how the Honey-bee got along before it had either the function or the Instinct, both of which now seem essential to its very existence? Then we have also to observe that it is the neuter bees that secrete the wax and build the cells; and since these neuter bees are sterile, the characteristics they possess and the skill they acquire, cannot be transmitted. All the bees that build cells and gather honey, have descended for thousands of years, at least, from parents that never did any thing of the kind.

Now this, Mr. Darwin would probably say, is a case of correlation.* That is, it is true the parents do not do these things, but these powers of the neuters are so correlated to the needs of the community, that the whole species become good builders by Natural Selection, because those swarms alone are preserved where such neuters are produced as get along with little wax and consequently with little

* "Origin of Species," 5th Am. Ed., pp. 227, 228.

loss of honey. He makes his explanation of the existence of the Instinct that constructs hexagonal cells, all turn on the fact that the bees must live over the winter.

But let us consider the work of the Wasps in the light of this theory. They do not use up honey in making their cells, and they do not live over the winter, so that Natural Selection has no chance to preserve the best builders through any such means as might be urged in the case of the Honey-bee. The Wasps perish every fall, excepting a few fertile females that desert the nest and live in some hiding-place, as we have before explained, to commence the new colonies the next year; and yet several species of Wasps and Hornets build six-sided cells, like the Honey-bee.

There is nothing here that aids at all, in the selection theory, even as Mr. Darwin has attempted to apply it to the Honey-bee.* Both of the means through which he attempts to show that Natural Selection acts in saving skilful builders,—the saving of honey in making cells of the best pattern and the necessity of the honey so saved, for winter use, —are here wanting; and yet the Wasps are as skilful mathematicians as though the existence of the species depended upon the angle of the cell!

The plain truth is, we have Bees and Wasps building in many different ways. Each method is connected with a peculiar structure and a whole train of Instincts. Besides, the whole doctrine of correlation, that seems to be solely relied upon to

* "Origin of Species," 5th Am. Ed., pp. 223, 224.

explain the perfection of the different kinds of insects found in such communities as we have described, has no sort of application to the slave Ants. They do their work perfectly, supplementing the defective organization and Instincts of their masters; but they are neuters, and never reproduce their kind! and the communities from which they are stolen cannot be affected in any way by the stealing of their young, so as to cause them to produce this remarkable set of slaves just fitted in structure and Instinct to do the work which their captors must have done for them, in order to live.

While acknowledging the powerful influence of Natural Selection in preserving the fittest, if we were called upon to work out a problem in creation that should make the belief in the origin of species by Natural Selection impossible, we should be unable to suggest a single change in the relation of the social insects as a whole, that would make a stronger case against such an origin of the species than we have in the relations now existing in many of the communities already considered. These relations seem to us more opposed to the theory of origin of species through selection, than any thing found in the physical organization of man even; and in reference to the human species, Mr. Wallace, one of the originators of the theory, acknowledges that it fails to satisfy him fully.*

There is no dispute about the facts—no dispute about the fact of variation, no dispute about the important influence of Natural Selection. But that

* "Natural Selection," pp. 332–350.

any given result in animal life, such as is seen in the complex societies of social insects, can be accomplished by these agencies working even for untold ages, does not follow. Some results may follow, but they must be such as these agencies have some competency to produce; and we must have some reasonable account of the *origin* of certain elements of the animal economy, as well as of their modification. But it is asked at once, If you grant "accidental variation" *and indefinite periods of time for the work of selection, have you not the elements of working out any supposable result? We answer, No. We can understand that a painter by throwing his sponge, in anger or desperation, upon his picture, might accidentally paint the foam upon the mouth of the dog with a naturalness that his pencil had failed to give. We can believe that this has been done. But now if we were told that a picture, like one of Landseer's or Rosa Bonheur's, could be made by throwing paint sponges against a canvas an indefinite number of times, we should not believe it; even if the experiment could be tried every day for millions of years. And although we can

* We use the words "*accidental variation,*" to signify any change that may occur in an organic being under new conditions—any change not specially provided for in his plan of development—any change by which individuals depart from the normal type of the species. It is in this way that we understood Mr. Darwin to use the words, and in the same way, we understand Mr. Wright to use them, in his defence of Darwin, written since these Lectures were delivered. (North Am. Rev., July 1871.) No one who understands Mr. Darwin, would accuse him of using the word "accidental" in any such sense as to imply any denial of causality.

readily believe that type might be so thrown by accident as to form a word, we could not on that account believe that a single page could be printed in that way, making an intelligent story, even if the experiment could be tried every day for a geologic age. If it is said we ought to believe in such results, from the elements of variation and indefinite time, we cannot help it. We are satisfied that with the same data to rely upon, all men will not reach the same conclusions. It is possible that this may be partly the result of training, and it may arise from a constitutional difference among men in weighing proof. Probably we shall have to wait a long time for Natural Selection to give us a race of men, who shall have powers of observation and reasoning so nearly alike, that they shall all reach the same results on such subjects. In the mean time, it becomes every one, who treats of such subjects at all, to make sure of his facts, to meekly follow any theory sustained by the facts, and resolutely oppose any, that seems to him inconsistent with them.

LECTURE VII.

INSTINCT CONNECTED WITH THE PARENTAL RELATION.—AS DEMANDING CERTAIN CHANGES IN OTHER ANIMALS AND PLANTS.—AS A LAW FOR THE ANIMAL.—AS SUBJECT TO VARIATION.

Effect of Parental Instinct.—Completes its course.—Disturbed by Domestication.—Answering Instinct of the young.—Correlation of the three kingdoms of Nature.—Hibernation.—Gall-flies.—Ichneumon-flies.—Bot-fly.—Tent-moth.—Oak-pruners.—Borer.—Preservation of the fittest.—Instinct as a Law.—Uniformity among Animals.—Periodicity and Self-regulating power of the Appetites.—Instinct can be deceived.—Follows the impression of the senses.—Variation of Instinct.—Production of varieties.—Definition of an Instinct, and of Instinct as a general term.

WE have already referred, incidentally, to some of the manifestations of Instinct connected with the parental relation. But there is in this relation, so much of antagonism to common instincts, as to make it worthy of separate consideration.

In many cases, the character of the animal, while it has young, seems to be entirely changed. Often the most timid animals become brave in defence of their offspring, and the welfare of the individual is sacrificed for the good of the species. We may announce it as the general law of all the instincts connected with the reproduction of young, that they are exercised at the expense of the individual. In the case of some of the lower animals, as insects, this effect is so marked that death almost immediately follows, after provision has been made for the continuance of the species. And among mammals of every grade, not only is the production of young a draft upon the animal powers, but the maintenance and defence of the young, lead animals to encounter many dangers, to which they would not otherwise be exposed. The instinctive love of life, even, is often held in abeyance, by the instinctive love of offspring; so that animals expose themselves to death, in defence of their young.

This instinct, that leads to the care of the young, continues in full force while they need the care. But in the case of some animals, that have been carefully observed, it has been found that there comes a time, when this instinct is reversed, so to speak,—when the mother will drive from her the young, which, a few days before, she would have risked her life in defence of. It is interesting to see the entire change that takes place, sometimes, in a single day. As long as the hen appears with ruffled feathers and an angry sounding cluck, she is ready to fight for her chickens; but all of a sudden, her feathers are smooth, her voice changes from the cluck to a musical note; and then she fiercely drives her young from her. Her Instinct has now completed its round. Every peculiar instinct of motherhood appeared, as the production of young and their protection required it. Each one appeared in connection with certain bodily functions, over which she had no control. When the functions ceased, the special instincts ceased with them. Her Instinct is, henceforth, exercised in the constant labor of self-protection and self-support, till a new round of duties begin, with the making of a new nest.

In the unnatural conditions under which many of our domestic animals are kept, this instinct, that leads to the production and care of young, is apparently modified, or kept in abeyance, by some stronger instinct or change of function, that we do not understand. Certain animals, as Elephants and Eagles, never produce young while under the control of man; and in other cases, certain instincts, that continue to act to some extent, are weakened and rendered irregular in their action; as in the case of fowls, which produce eggs, but never brood; and sheep that will not own their young.

When we consider how dependent Instinct is upon function, and know how domestication interferes with the natural habits of animals, and also that the selection exercised by man, often comes in to secure conditions of life that never would occur under the influence of Natural Selection, we shall be prepared to find many seeming anomalies of Instinct among our domestic animals. These anomalies may give us important information, as to the original habits of these animals, or as to the plasticity of their natures in the hand of man. There is now, in Natural History, no more interesting field of observation than that offered by our domestic animals,—no one, that promises more advantage to science, or to the money interests of the community. But of the variation of Instinct under domestication and its relation to man, we shall have occasion to speak again.

All Instinct, on the part of many animals, would be useless in providing for their young, were there not an answering Instinct on the part of the young, that brings them into proper relation to their parents, or to the world, in those cases where parental care cannot avail for them.

The cry of danger, from the hen or partridge, would be of no avail to save her scattered brood, were there not an answering Instinct in the young, that instantly recognizes the note of warning, and impels them to seek cover. They fly *from* the mother and hide themselves; as though conscious that she cannot protect them from the bird of prey, without exposing herself to death.

Among our highest domestic animals, the mammals, the care of the dam would fail to provide for the young, were there not an Instinct which leads the young to seek the udder. Here is the milk secreted; and it is the food, and the only proper food, for the young. And they seek it for themselves; for not one of these hoof-bearing mammals, could feed its own young; or, in any direct way, aid the young in feeding; and the same is true of wild animals, that have the same structure. The young of such animals, must feed themselves, without aid or instruction. They must feed themselves at once, or die. There never was a time when those animals could care better for their young than now. Their very existence is proof of Instinct as a gift, and not as the result of experience,—an Instinct, as perfect in the beginning as now; for an experience, without the Instinct first given as a condition, is impossible, from the very structure of those hoof-bearing tribes, which can give their young no aid whatever, in securing food.

Among birds, as we have noticed in another connection, we have beautiful examples of the instinct of the young responsive to the instinct of the mother. Many birds are hatched in a very immature state. They can neither fly, nor walk, nor see. All they have strength to do, is to raise the head and open the bill; and this they all do every time the mother lights upon the nest. They do it at once; it is all they need to do; but this they must do, or die. There is no time for them to learn by experience,—they must be ready to do the *right thing at once, of their own accord.* And there was no better chance for any ancestor to learn by experience. This habit, common to all kinds of young birds hatched in an immature state, could not be an acquired habit; but must be something given as independently of any agency of ancestors, as the growth of bone or the arrangement of muscles.

A marvellous thing it is, that the mother bird, when the brood is numerous, should be able rightly to divide her favors. If she is guided by sight at all, there must be wonderful acuteness of vision, that enables Woodpeckers and Wrens, in their covered nests, and Kingfishers and Bank-swallows, in their deep holes in the earth, to discern one of their young from the other.

Although there is much connected with this subject that we cannot understand, there are certain facts, such as we have referred to, plain to every observer, showing a wonderful correlation of instinctive action between the parent and its young.

This correlation commences immediately on the hatching of the young bird, and it is common to thousands of kinds of birds, under a variety of conditions.

Many illustrations of the same principle can be found among the invertebrate animals; and with some of them, this principle of correlation of Instinct is of wider application,—a third element often comes in to act, as will appear in considering the following topics:

1. *Instinct of animals requiring certain changes in other kinds of animals, or in plants, for the completion of its work.*

2. *The peculiar instinct of one stage of being as preparatory to another, in which that instinct is entirely lost; as in the case of many insects.*

Every plant has certain relations to the inorganic world, as we have pointed out in a previous lecture. There is a correlation of its changes and developments, both as to time and conditions required for them, with the changes in the inorganic world.

The animal kingdom, as a whole, not only depends upon the vegetable, but it is fitted to the vegetable kingdom, in many respects, as that is related to the inorganic world. Important physiological changes in animals, as well as change of instinct, or rather quickening of instinct in special directions, correspond with certain changes in the vegetable kingdom; without which, these changes in the animals would be meaningless, useless, or even destructive to them.

The animals that hibernate, find food, such as they use, most abundant in the fall; and at the same time, there seems to be a physiological change, by which the animal lays up an extra store of fat in its tissues, to keep the lamp of life burning during winter. If this change is not provided for in the animal's system, by physiological action, then he has the Instinct to hoard food, and has activity enough in winter to live upon it. The instincts of migratory birds, change with the season; some of them returning while snow and ice are abundant; so that they are evidently driven north by a quickened instinct, rather than enticed by green fields and sunny skies.

All the birds bring forth their young at that season when their food is abundant, and when there will be time for the young brood to mature, before the change of season can make its demand upon them. The wild goose must make her way to the lakes of the far north, in season to rear her brood, and have them full fledged and strong of wing to join in that grand procession towards the south, in autumn.

All these adjustments, by which the animal kingdom struggles successfully for existence, depend upon the fact that the quickening of functions, and of special instincts needful to carry on the work to completion, correspond with the changes in the inorganic world and vegetable kingdom.

These general adaptations of living things to the changes of the earth, and the correlation of the changes among the different orders of living things, are much more common and marked than is generally supposed. Every change seems to be a part of a series of machinery adjusted and set in motion according to a plan; and such a plan, that every wheel must move with a given velocity, and start and stop at a given time, or loss and ruin follow.

But in addition to these general adaptations, by which all beings in the world seem to be more or less dependent upon others, there are certain special relations of animals to plants and of animals to each other, secured by Instinct, that strike us in the same manner, as special structure in animals and plants themselves. There is a whole tribe of insects, to which we have before referred, that make galls upon plants, or check the growth of the axis of plants in some peculiar manner. The Gall-fly deposits an egg upon the leaf or twig, according to her habit; and then her work ceases. Now the tree takes up the work—forms a house for the young insect and provides it with food; until, at last, the perfect insect makes its way through the walls of the house, into the open air. This is an entirely different thing from those many cases, where the egg is simply deposited so that the young can find proper food; as in the case of the Tent-moth, that deposits eggs upon Apple or Cherry twigs; or of the Carrion-fly, which deposits her eggs upon flesh or fish. The action of securing food, in both of the latter cases, is entirely on the part of the young insects; that is, they simply eat the substance as they find it, though not specially prepared for them, as the Oak-gall is, for its inhabitant. The Apple-trees are sufferers only in the loss of leaves destroyed, before they have done their work for the trees. There is no evidence of any relation of the tree to the insect, except as being its appropriate food, and in putting out its leaves at the right time; that is, before the eggs of the insect hatch. But in the case of the Oaks, the Roses, the Spruces and Golden-rods, and many other plants, there is a positive marshalling of the powers of the plants to provide both food and lodging for the young insect. And they do this work in as regular a manner as they form leaves or flowers.

These plants act as foster-parents; and in supplementing the work of the parent insect, they perform the exact office of working bees in the Honey-bee hive.

There are ichneumon insects, and parasitic flies, that sting the caterpillars of certain moths, but do it in such a way that the caterpillar lives and eats, until his enemies have come to maturity at the expense of his life; or, at least, of his power to rise into a higher life. It is no uncommon thing for a collector to find a caterpillar bearing numerous small cocoons;—the work of his enemies, that have wasted his life,—or to open a cocoon, and in place of the chrysalis, to find very many smaller objects: the young of insects, which have been provided for by the joint products of the body and instinct of the cocoon-builder. The parasites fed upon the chrysalis of the insect, and they were protected, during their transformation, by the cocoon which he had prepared for his own transformation.

The common Bot-fly is another example of the dependence of one animal upon another, for the completion of the work, which its Instinct has begun. This fly deposits her egg upon the hair of the horse, where it is held by a glue that instantly hardens. If the work were left where the mother leaves it, there would soon be an end of the species. But she deposits her eggs, instinctively, on such parts of the body of the horse that he will swallow more or less of them. When the eggs or *larvæ* have reached the horse's stomach, they have found the proper place for development,—a place which the insect mother cannot reach, and having no connection with the parts where the eggs are deposited. But the fly, as though understanding the whole process and the calculation of chances, puts her eggs in such a position, that enough of them shall reach their place of development, to keep the species good.

The wonderful processes by which the *entozoa* find their appropriate place of development, in all their stages of growth, are analogous to this; but are too intricate for use here as illustrations.

We have in the Bot-fly, another manifestation of Instinct, that is difficult to be reconciled with that theory which resolves it into fixed habits formed by the experience of past generations; or to tendencies inherited through any means. The egg is deposited by the mother, and she soon dies. It is then removed to the stomach of the horse, where it wakes to life and spends the first stage of its existence. It has never had any connection with the leg of a horse, except as an egg. Before it comes into the world, to act as a fly, all the former race of Bot-flies are dead. It must begin its work for itself; and it goes, not where it began life, for that is impossible; but, to the place where it was deposited as an egg. So if we refer Instinct, in this case, to experience in the present race or past races, the experience begun and treasured up, must have begun in the egg!

We have a multitude of examples, of instinct of this kind, which moves on changing, as the young changes from the egg to maturity; with no parental care to aid it, and no parental example for imitation.

The eggs of the Tent-moth are its only representatives in the spring of the year. But the thousands of young insects from these eggs, all start off in the work of feeding and web-weaving and migrating from the web, and cocoon building, just as all others of the same kind have done every year before. And yet, no parent has ever seen its young, and no young has ever seen a parent, or any of its works.

The Oak-pruners deposit their eggs on the branches of the oak; and the young insect grows and cares for itself until the proper time comes for its transformation. Then it cuts the limb between itself and the tree, so that its branch may fall to the earth, where it goes through its transformations. All the thousands do exactly the same things, as all previous generations have done before them.

The Apple-tree Borer deposits her egg in the bark and there leaves it. The Borer mines in the wood, feeding and growing for months. But before the time of transformation, it prepares its hole, so that it can easily escape into a world, where it has never been, and from which, up to that time, it has tried to escape. It has never seen the outer world nor known a parent's care, nor one of its kind ; but it comes forth fitted for its work, not only by structure but by Instinct to guide,—to guide it perfectly, in entirely new relations to the world, and in the use of organs it never before possessed. The being bursts into life with nothing to learn, fully prepared to act its part,—and it is absolutely necessary that it should be thus provided for; because it has neither the time nor the conditions for obtaining its needful knowledge, as intelligent beings must obtain theirs.

It is plain, from these cases and the hundreds like them, which might be cited, that animals come into the world with all their instinctive capacities ready for action, the instant they are needed. And this instinctive outfit, being essential at once to the continuance of life, could not have been acquired by any changes resulting from experience or observation, by themselves or their ancestors.

The instinct of the young is supplemented, in many cases, it is true, by the instinct of the parent.

But in those species, where the young is thrown upon the world without a parent's care, its Instinct is sufficient to guide it, the instant it is hatched. And the Instinct develops as a guide to the animal, just as his organs become fitted for action. The Instinct, in every case, changes as the conditions of life change by development; whether the changes are gradual or sudden,—so that the most complex and wonderful manifestations of these original principles of action, are found among the lower tribes of the animal kingdom. Multitudes of insects commence life in the earth and in the water. Some of them spend years, mining in the ground, or hiding among the rocks and mud of brooks and lakes. They have organs and instincts that fit them for such life. But the day comes, when they suddenly pass to a higher life of the air. There is oftentimes as complete change of instincts, as of organs,—but both are just fitted for the new life of their possessor; each supplementing the other. The machine and guiding power are ready at the same time.

When, now, appeal is made to the "*preservation of the fittest,*" amidst infinite variation of forms, as accounting for the present perfection of relation among all these beings, to each other, and to the world, in which they live, we reply, as in a former lecture, that we are in want of some fitness to *begin with;* before there can be variation, and the "fittest" be preserved. Preservation is one thing,—the production of something to be preserved, is another,—especially, where the thing preserved can be preserved only by means of its own characteristics—through its own struggle for existence.

We are now prepared to see in what respect *Instinct is a law for the animal.*

We have seen from our discussions thus far, that something must be given to every animal as its outfit in starting in the world. There must be not only impulse, but there must be a certain amount of knowledge and skill possessed by the animal, when it just comes into the world, just as necessarily as it must have a stomach and lungs. If any object to the terms, knowledge and skill, because the capabilities are not acquired, they cannot deny the existence in animals of these capabilities, that take the place of acquired knowledge and skill among men.

I conceive that the knowledge and skill, which the young animal comes into the world with, differ no more from that which he gains in after life, from experience, than his stomach and lungs at the first moment of life differ from the same organs after they have grown by the process of taking food. The young animal comes into the world with organs all fitted for a certain work, and with knowledge and skill to fit him for that work,—that is, to maintain his place in the world. Nature seems to give him, at birth, as little as possible of both bodily and mental powers; using the word mental as including all the activities involving volition. But she acts wisely, and gives the animal bodily and mental powers sufficient for the conditions in which it first wakes to life. If it is to have a parent's care, then it has powers of body and mind just sufficient to supplement the parent's labors. If it is one of a race which never see their parents, then it has greater gifts to begin with; and fights its own battles, from the first moment of conscious existence. It knows how to meet any emergency and perform every needful work, as well as though instructed in the best polytechnic schools, and aided by a century of experience.

When we consider the whole history of animals, one of the first things that strikes us, is the great uniformity that appears among those of the same kind, when left to themselves under favoring conditions. When we compare animals with the human species, we see a uniformity in all the manifestations of being, on the one side, that could be secured only by a controlling force, uniform in its nature and operations in each species; and on the other, a diversity, that seems to originate from a force having some peculiarity in every individual case. It is a matter of great interest to trace the cause of this uniformity on the one hand, and of this diversity, on the other; and to this investigation the remaining lectures will be chiefly devoted.

But for the present we wish to consider briefly the uniformity of individuals in the same species of animals; and leave the question of diversity among men, even of the same family, for future consideration, when we have more materials bearing upon the subject.

We have already seen that Instinct, in its simplest form, supplements structure and function; and that Instinct varies in every animal, as the structure and function of his organs change. These three elements then being the same in thousands of individuals of the same species, we shall have a constant resultant in each one of them, unless external circumstances come in as a disturbing element. These three elements are so strong in their combined action, in every animal, that they shape his life,—experience is not able to turn him from the course along which they impel him. Experience may do much for the higher animals,—it may keep them from danger, add to their enjoyment of life and improve them in many ways; but it can never turn them from that course, along which the functions of organs and the original impulse and guidance of Instinct, carry them.

We see nothing in animals of the same species, that renders them unlike each other in following the impulses arising from the function of their organs.—The animal seems, in this respect, to be passive in the formation of its controlling impulses; and he follows the great impulses of his nature, freely, and without consideration of the remote consequences. That nature of the animal, which leads him to take into consideration only the present, the surrounding circumstances for the moment, will secure a uniformity not to be expected in man, who brings in to modify every activity, the memory of the past, the accumulated experience of men in all ages, and the expectation of the future, with all its uncertainties, which never can affect an animal, since they cannot be comprehended by him. Just in proportion as we find men leaving out of consideration the experience of the past and the prospects of the future, do we find almost a brute-like uniformity of action among them; as is seen in the lowest savage tribes; and just in proportion as we see among animals, any mingling of the memories of the past with their present impressions, do we see a want of uniform action among members of the same species. All that we can then say is, that in animals, structure, function, and that part of Instinct which supplements them, are so strong that they move on together, giving the same results in all animals of the same species; or so nearly the same results, that the changes produced in instinctive life by experience, as peculiar to each animal, are as the perturbations of the planets in their course, so small that they do not interfere with the general result; and unless the perturbation occurs in the same quarter and is often repeated, it never accumulates to a sum sufficient to attract attention, except by the most careful inspection. We speak now of animals in their free state; and not of that abnormal condition to which the influence of man may reduce them.

The result is uniform, because all the influences of experience are, with animals, mainly subordinate to that high wisdom, which we call Instinct; a wisdom given to the animal for his guidance, doing the work which the human race can do only by hard experience and patient thought. When will man reach like uniform and happy results for himself, through that free Intelligence, by which he must guide himself, or fall below the brutes?

As a means of rendering results almost mechanically uniform among animals, even when they follow their impulses, we find the most important functions only periodically active; and so far as we know, no harm comes to one animal more than to another, while in his natural state, from following the impulse of his appetites to the full extent of their demand. He can be deceived, as we shall show; but he is injured by being deceived, thus gratifying his appetite on the wrong substance, and not because he indulged his appetite to too great an extent.

In man, the appetites have but a slight self-regulating power,—they need control and restraint from their possessor,—while among animals they are perfectly self-regulating by the periodicity and strength of the functions that originate them. And as instinctive action, so far as the appetites are concerned, simply supplements function, of course it never goes beyond the proper bound; because the appetite gives it no occasion for going beyond that bound.

What we mean then when we say that Instinct is a law for the animal is, that those original principles of action in him, which were given as his first outfit in life, always control him in the main; experience doing but little in directing the course of life, though it may do much in conducting it to a successful issue in that course. The instinctive principles guide the animal in its action, to that which

crystal of salt which is poison to her, and eats it, mistaking it for the grain of quartz, that is necessary to her, for the process of digestion. Here the Instinct of eating gravel, which is very curious in itself, is linked to a certain impression upon the sense of sight.

The whole process of cheating animals to capture them, depends upon the fact that the purely *instinctive* notions of the animal, arise from a certain relation of external objects to its senses; as truly as those notions that may come to it in consequence of experience. The sense of smell is the occasion of mistake by the fly; the sense of sight, of mistake by the fowl, when she swallows salt instead of gravel; and she is deceived by the sense of hearing, when she hides at the cry, like that of the hawk, though the sound may be made by a mocking-bird, or by man. These are only examples; many of which will occur to every observer. Those given are enough to show that Instinct does not correct the senses, or render them more acute; but that instinctive acts, such as we have mentioned, always have a certain relation to the impressions made upon the senses. Many of the mistakes of Instinct, so called, are the indications that we have in many acts, especially among the higher animals, something more than Instinct,—at least, a limited range of that principle of Intelligence belonging peculiarly to man, which works out the noblest results, but is liable to mistakes, until rendered safe in its action by long experience.

If Instinct is the controller of animal activity,

the question naturally arises, How far, and under what conditions is it subject to variation?

There is a tendency in almost all plants and animals, if not in all, to vary from one exact type, giving rise to varieties. The extent to which this variation may go, is at present one of the disputed points among naturalists, and one which it is very difficult to settle. All readily acknowledge that species vary so as to give a multitude of varieties; as in the case of the common apple and other cultivated fruits; while some hold to the distinct origin of species themselves, and others regard them as simply permanent, well marked varieties.

Without entering into this discussion fully, which our present purpose does not require, there are certain things in regard to this variation of species, upon which most naturalists seem to be agreed.

1. Variation may take place in any plant or animal in a manner and from causes quite beyond our comprehension; that is, apparently from some original constitution of the being.

2. Rapid variation is in general, most common among the higher groups of plants and animals; especially among those most useful to man.

3. When the process of variation has commenced in any kind, we naturally expect from our observation, that instances of variation in that kind will become increasingly common.

This may explain the reason for our finding so much variation among our best cultivated plants and domestic animals. They have been under the influence of man so long, and so many new forms have been preserved, that permanent characteristics are not to be expected; as in nature, where only those types are preserved, which can fight their own battles in the world.

4. There is a tendency for any characteristic, brought out by variation, to be propagated and finally to become fixed, so that it is sure to appear in the young of the parent possessing that characteristic.

The tendency to exhibit peculiar characteristics, is, perhaps, most marked, or, at least, most noticeable, in respect to size and color. But there are great variations in the super-sensuous nature of animals. Docility, viciousness, stupidity, and most other characteristics, that we see in different degrees among men, we also see in different degrees, among animals of the same species. And these characteristics are as likely to be transmitted, as is peculiarity of form or color.

But docility, viciousness and stupidity are not instincts at all. They simply mark qualities of the instincts, or their degree of perfection; if they can be referred to Instinct at all. We believe that those qualities belong chiefly, if not wholly, to Intelligence, or the capacity of the animal to understand the relation of his acts as means to ends. Certain it is, that by training and care in selection, we can secure habits or tendencies in breeds of animals, as well as we can secure difference of form. In this respect, we see no difference between men and animals. Men vary in the powers of mind,—even members of the same family are often quite unlike in temper, taste and ability. But we do not speak of this difference among men, as any proof that one possesses powers, in kind, that the other does not possess; but that one possesses a degree of power and quality of temper which the other does not have.

There has been much confusion in reasoning, in regard to the super-sensuous nature of animals, because so many have decided, at the outset, that they are here in a field entirely different from that found in the study of man; and because qualities of powers or faculties, have been treated as new powers, or as something having a tendency to produce new powers. Qualities may give the being new *power*, but not new *powers* or *faculties*. The new power comes from the better use and greater strength of old powers.

But in addition to these qualities that make a difference between individuals of the same species, and which vary in the same individual, in different periods of life, we have taught in these lectures, that Instinct varies in its manifestations in the same individual to meet the different conditions of life; as plants vary by the law of their growth, for the same purpose. That original impulse, knowledge and skill, which are possessed by the animal without experience, and which we have called INSTINCT, are excited to action by the circumstances in which the animal is placed. It often happens, that an animal is so situated that it lives easily by the exercise of only a part of this original gift; while a change of circumstances will instantly call the rest of the knowledge and skill into play. Those who see the change for the first time, wonder at what seems to them manifestations of wisdom on the part of the actor. Mistakes have been made in the study of animals, from want of careful observation in regard to the nature and conditions of such changes in instinctive action.

It is probable that instincts may be strengthened in certain directions, and weakened in others, and changed in quality. If this cannot be done directly, it certainly can be done indirectly, by affecting the functions of the body, which are the chief agencies in bringing the instincts into play, and affecting their strength and quality.

There is great plasticity in the organic and super-sensuous part of the lower tribes even; sufficient to give them a fair chance in the world; and when we come to the higher animals, we have a still greater plasticity of nature; so that qualities and habits can be secured and transmitted, as tendencies at least, from one generation to another.

This is so well understood by breeders that they will, in time, secure almost any form or color which they desire,—not because they have any power to change these directly, but because they take advantage of the tendency in all animals to vary and to inherit the peculiarities of parents. In like manner, any peculiar manifestation of an instinct can be fixed by selection in breeding. The breeder is attracted by some habit of an animal, which would be desirable. That is to him a hint. That animal is preserved; and the chances are that some of its young will manifest the same characteristics, perhaps in an increased degree. The selection goes on in this direction for generations,—every thing in other directions being rejected and every thing in that direction being preserved,—until the peculiar characteristic is fixed; sure to appear in every one of the variety or breed. This may explain the difference between Shepherd-dogs, Pointers, Bull-dogs and other breeds. It is not certain however, that all our dogs came from the same original stock.

It is to be noticed that this variation in Instinct, is according to a definite plan. Change of Instinct in strength or quality, seems to be accompanied with a corresponding change of structure. The two move on together, by some inscrutable law. The savage temper of the Bull-dog is accompanied with a ponderous jaw and enormous strength of muscle. The keen scent of the Blood-hound and the structure for running all harmonize with his instinct for following the prey. The Spaniel and Newfoundland dog readily take to the water; and their web-feet fit them for this element.

The Instinct, which leads the fowl to sit upon her eggs, is always connected with a peculiar physiological change in the body. That change seems first to awaken the instinct and bring it into play. There is an unnatural heat of the body,—a change in the temper of the fowl, and a disregard of danger. In fact, the whole nature of the animal seems to be changed by some law of its being, as its feathers grow or drop off, at particular seasons. This physiological change and the manifestation of the instinct to brood, come after a certain number of eggs are laid, called a "*nest*." But it has been found that these "*nests*" vary in number; and by continued selections, breeds have been secured that never brood. The valuable characteristic of constantly producing eggs, is secured; but there would be the loss of the breed, were it not for the care of man.

In consequence of the abnormal conditions, to which domestic animals are subjected, we must expect great confusion in the manifestations of their natural habits. There are great modifications of Instinct, as we find among dogs, modifications of the original Instinct, in particular directions, intensified by habit and rendered constant by careful breeding. There is no more difference in the Instinct of the different kinds of dogs, then there is in their structure. And as all the different forms of dogs are seen to be modifications of one type, so their instincts appear to be modifications of the normal instincts seen among those dogs which are supposed to be near the original type.

The relation of function to Instinct is much more intimate than is generally supposed, so that the action of one may be mistaken for that of the other. The wonderful instinct of the hound is often referred to as enabling him to track his prey, even upon the dry earth. It is not Instinct, at all, that enables him to do this. It is function,—the delicacy of the organ of smelling. He has the Instinct to follow his prey, as the common dogs have, but he is able to follow his prey when they are baffled, only by a more delicate function of one special sense. Instinct leads the common dog to hunt for his master's track; but it is function that enables him to find it.

All the reciprocal influences of structure, function and Instinct on the being, under the varied conditions to which our domestic animals are subjected, will never be understood until they have been studied long, with great care. It is in this field of observation, that we look for the most interesting results, in determining the limits of variation in the whole structure and nature of the animal. Conceding the great changes that have taken place in the modifying of forms and Instincts, we see nothing yet that indicates the production of a new Instinct; and we can never be sure that an instinct is lost simply because it does not act. An instinct may lie dormant for generations because there is no occasion for its activity; but sheep warn their fellows of danger, and cows hide their calves when the occasion comes for calling the old instincts into play. And the calf, stupid as he is, knows his part of the perförmance in hiding, as well as though trained in the best schools!

We have thus seen the wide application of these spontaneous activities. They increase in number and complexity according to the nature of the beings in which they appear. They appear when they are needed, and they pass away when there is no longer use for them. They save the individual and the species; and this they do by working wonders; but if they did not perform these wonders; the species could not exist, as they are.

Each step makes it plainer to us, that we have not here a distinct principle or an agent, as Hamilton calls it;* but that *an Instinct is simply an impulse to a particular kind of voluntary action which the being needs to perform as an individual or representative of a species; but which he could not possibly learn to perform before he needs to act.* And the general term, INSTINCT, *includes all the original impulses,—excepting the Appetites,—and that knowledge and skill, with which animals are endowed—which experience may call into exercise, but which it does not give.*

All of these are given to an animal in proportion to his need—according to the conditions under which he is to start in life; and not at all in proportion to his rank in the scale of being. And all attempts to fix the rank of an animal by means of the number and perfection of those principles of action, utterly fail. It is just as logical to argue that a Sea-urchin is nearly allied to man in structure, because his spines have ball and socket joints, like the limbs of man, as to argue that an animal is near man in Intelligence, because his instinctive acts imitate the intelligent acts of man.

If we accept the account thus far given of the nature of instinctive acts, we must be prepared to recognize Intelligence as reaching much lower in the scale of being than it has generally been supposed that it does. And by intelligence, we mean

* Metaphysics, Bowen's Ed., p. 505.

here, simply, the power in the actor of comprehending ends as desirable, and his own acts as means to secure those ends. Intelligence carries on the work by experience which was begun by Instinct. An intelligent act can be distinguished from an instinctive act only by the conditions under which it is performed. They may both be exactly the same in form and in their relation to ends.

LECTURE VIII.

HIGHER CHARACTER OF ANIMALS.—ANIMALS COMPARED WITH MAN.

Knowledge from Experience.—Do animals think?—Definition of thinking.—Conditions of the act to be studied.—Difficulty of the work.—Condition of the animal.—Physical structure and growth in Men and Animals.—The Senses in both.—Physiological likeness.—Capacity of Animals for Pain and Enjoyment.—Psychological effects of sensations in Animals.—Fear, Anger, Joy, Grief, Shame.—The Desires.—Æsthetic nature of Animals.—Animals learn by experience.—Their actions compared with those of man.—Taming and trapping Animals.—Memory of Animals.—Dreaming.—Summary of the Argument.—Instinct the controlling power.—The Rights of Animals.

ANIMALS are plainly guided by some principle of voluntary action, which secures complicated results necessary for their well-being, before they can have experience, or instruction. These voluntary activities, rising above the functional activities, but working in harmony with them, without experience, or instruction, on the part of their possessor, secure the welfare of the individual, and the continuance of the species. These activities, taken together, constitute INSTINCT; as that word is generally understood. And Instinct, as thus defined, is undoubtedly the sole guide of many of the lower tribes. We judge so, because they do not appear to have the conditions for an experience; and yet they accomplish their work perfectly, and in the same manner, wherever found. But so far as experience is possible, the animal seems to be as dependent upon that, as is the human race itself.

The self-directive, voluntary activities seem to be confined, in every species, to the narrowest sphere of action possible, consistent with the welfare of each species, under its ordinary conditions of life.

In addition to those actions which are plainly instinctive,—because performed at once, in the same manner, by all members of any given species,—we see animals performing other acts, in the same line, or connected with them, that seem plainly to depend upon acquired knowledge.

We perform the same kinds of acts, as many animals perform, not only because we have been taught by others, who have also been taught or aided by experience, but we do them understandingly: comprehending the relations of means to ends; *knowing*, *feeling*, *willing*. We form plans, and execute them for our pleasure. The mistakes of inexperience, we correct by observation; and we daily become more skilful in any work we do. All these acts and results mark us as "thinking beings," as this phrase is generally understood. Within certain limits, the higher animals appear to learn by the same process as we do, and to act with the same comprehension of means and ends. The duestion then naturally arises, Do any animals possess a mental, or super-sensuous, organization like that of a man, in kind; so that any of their acts, are the result of choice, as related to some end comprehended by them as desirable? In other words, do animals comprehend relations, and then act for the purpose of securing pleasure, by adapting means to ends; or are they impelled to all acts, for their preservation and productive of pleasure to them, by a blindly working force, that gives law to their voluntary acts, with no aid from any of those powers, that are the chief distinction of man? Are animals, in any proper sense, thinking beings? The answer to this question can be given, not by considering the nature of any act alone, but the conditions, under which the act is performed. For purely instinctive acts manifest as much wisdom, as any intelligent act possibly can, in aiming at the same result. We must also agree as to what is meant by *thinking;* or else, while we agree as to the mental status of animals, we may continue our war of words, simply in defence of our definitions.

We have had of late, the question proposed; What is it to think? And we have had answers given, that all thought involves processes beyond the powers of animals, and therefore that they do not think. This is a short way of disposing of the matter; and most questions can be disposed of in the same manner. If a man starts with a given definition of thinking, declaring that it always involves certain elements, and then denies that animals ever have those elements, because he accounts for all apparent manifestation of these elements in them, by some low form of association of ideas, the argument, with him, is ended, of course. We believe that animals have elements of thought, which some have denied to them. We know, certainly, that animals act as though they had notions of time, space and causality. But it can never be conclusively proved that they have them, we readily admit.

To be explicit, let us define "thinking," as we now intend to use the word. If any object to the definition, they will understand our meaning. When any being performs an act, to secure pleasure or avoid pain, because he comprehends his act as a means to secure the end, we consider that *thinking* is involved,—of course, it often rises into higher planes than this, as philosophical thinking; but we consider that it begins, wherever beings act from any *comprehension* of *means and ends*.

That animals perform acts, which seem to imply thought, no one will deny; purely instinctive acts, and even the movements of plants, seem to imply thought, where there is no sensation even. If we detect Intellect in animals at all then, it will not be, because they perform certain acts; but it will be, because they perform these acts under the same conditions, and by the same means, or methods, as men perform them. We must direct our attention then, mainly to the conditions under which the acts of the higher animals are performed.

We are now called upon to enter one of the most difficult of all fields of observation, and to compare objects that elude the grasp of every sense. Those who have attempted to compare their own sensations and conceptions with those of others, know how difficult the work is. Even in regard to our sensations, or sense-perceptions, we can never be sure that ours correspond with those of another person, under the same conditions. You and your friend look at a flower, and agree that it is yellow; but it does not follow that you both have the same color-sensation. It simply follows, that each of you has the same sensation, that has been produced in him, by all objects which he has been taught to call, yellow. But, as a matter of fact, when your friend says he perceives a yellow color, he may have just the same sensation, as you have, when you call the color, blue. It is not probable that it is so, but it is not possible for the best physicist, or metaphysician in the world, to so make the comparison, as to be sure that two persons have sensations alike, when they give the same name to the sensations. There is, indeed, one strong argument against the likeness of sensations, which bear the same name, in different individuals; that is, the different effect of these sensations upon the sensibilities. Two persons agree as to a color; but one likes it, another dislikes it. They agree as to the name of an odor or taste; but they disagree, as to the effect of that odor or taste, upon themselves. It is certainly a fair question; Does not the different effect of a taste, or odor, or color, on different individuals, imply that each produces a different sensation upon one person from what it does upon another? These inquiries are started here, to show the inherent difficulty of comparing the sensations and mental operations of different individuals, if one is disposed to be sceptical, or to insist upon absolute proof of their agreement or likeness, in any given case.

The proof of identity of sensations and sense-perceptions, can be only inferential, strengthened, indeed, by our belief in the uniformity, which we see running throughout our physical structures, so far as the examination can be made, by the aid of the senses.

Because animals cannot speak, it seems, at first thought, a more difficult thing to compare man with an animal, than it is to compare man with man. And so it is, in some respects; as the mental operations can best be revealed through language, and some of them, only in this way. But the difference, in the two cases, is by no means so great as it, at first, appears. We must in both cases, infer the correspondence of sensations and mental states, by certain effects. Man can aid us by language; but, on the other hand, an animal has no metaphysical theory that comes in to disturb his sensations, or his acts, as consequent upon those sensations. So it may fairly be assumed that the honesty of an animal, in acting free from all theories, and all knowledge that he is under examination, may be a fair offset against the gift of speech, as an aid in investigating the sensations and conceptions of our fellow-men.

As our object now is, to make a fair comparison of man with the highest and best known, of the lower animals, we begin with their bodies.

The structure of all vertebrates is essentially the same, and varied, only in accordance with the conditions of life, in each species. There is, also, likeness of substance. If we take a human bone and one from a dog, and analyze them, we find them, throughout of the same chemical composition. The bones grow, and the tissues are combined, in essentially the same manner in both. The differences are merely specific, but the generic character of bone is constant. If we compare the muscles of both, the same is true. Not only are the muscle of a dog and that of a man alike in their general structure, action and use, but they are composed of the same materials, and they grow in the same manner. The nervous systems of both have essentially the same composition, as they have the same structure and the same use. So, throughout, our comparison will hold, until we satisfy ourselves that, in any one of the higher vertebrate animals, we find the same kind of materials organized in the same manner, and for the same uses, as in our own bodies. Growth, decay, life and death are essentially the same, in all the higher animals, as in man.

Now let us advance a step, and compare the senses and sensations of both. We have no sense which we do not find in some animal; and the senses of animals, so far as we can judge, are affected in the same way as ours are, by the same objects. They may have some of the senses more acute than ours are, but they differ from ours, only in degree; as the senses of men differ in strength and delicacy. So far as we know, no animal has a sense that differs from ours, in kind.

If we examine the phenomena of the senses in

detail, we shall find the animal affected by colors, odors and sounds, as readily as men are. He may like what a man dislikes; as men may be affected, in different ways, by the same odor or taste. If we judge, as we do in every other case, it must be plain to every observer, that animals have the same kind of enjoyment and suffering, through the senses, as men have. To heat and cold, hunger and thirst, food and poison, sickness, pain and death, they have the same bodily relations, in kind, as we ourselves. So far as sensation has its recoil, in muscular or physiological effects, there is great similarity, if not identity, of effect.

Those, who deny that the lower animals suffer as men do, bring forward no valid argument in favor of their doctrine. It is clear assumption, from some notion of what they think ought to be,—a method of procedure utterly unworthy of any searcher for truth. Besides, they seem to forget that the same arguments, which are used to show that the dumb animals do not suffer, but only appear to suffer,—if accepted, would prove that these animals have no enjoyment, when they seem to be happy, but only manifest the appearance of happiness. So far as the argument, for the benevolence of Deity, is concerned, it seems quite as worthy of His character, that He has created the lower animals with the capacity for suffering and enjoyment, as that He has denied them both, and introduced a dumb show, that means nothing, simply to keep up appearances! We doubt not, the verdict of every thinking man, who takes time to study and observe, will be, that animals have great capacity for physical suffering and enjoyment; and that this capacity is greatest in those animals that are the companions of man, depending upon him for much of their enjoyment, and receiving from him, through ill temper, thoughtlessness, or neglect, the cause of almost the entire sum of their suffering. So perfectly adjusted do their powers seem to be, that, were they treated as well as we know how to treat them—though much remains to be learned of their proper treatment, as well as of our own,—their lives would be almost uninterrupted scenes of enjoyment; and they would contribute far more to the aid of man, than they now can. But let us now consider what may be called the psychological effects of sensations, as manifested, or made known to us, through the muscular and nervous systems.

An object known to man to be dangerous to him, or supposed to be dangerous, causes fear; and the emotion of fear has its natural language, which the whole body speaks. The emotion is manifested by a certain action of the muscles, producing a peculiar movement or fixedness of the eye, trembling, and unusual tones of voice. These same effects are all produced upon animals, by objects either dangerous to them, or to which they are unaccustomed. They are frightened, under exactly the same conditions as men are frightened; in many cases, by the same objects; and the effect of the fright upon them, as manifested by the muscular and nervous systems, is precisely the same as upon man,—and the actions of the animal, when he is frightened, have the same relation to his ordinary actions, as we observe in the case of men. We have intimated that animals know certain enemies, by a special instinct, such as men do not possess; but that question is not now under discussion. The question is, as to the animal's having the emotion of fear, from any cause; and as to the likeness of that emotion, to the emotion of fear in man.

Animals fear things that cannot injure them,—they judge, and very often misjudge. A horse is frightened at an old newspaper, fluttering in the street, or at a sudden light or sound, when no danger is near. He, to all appearances, has weak judgment. He, like man, tries to avoid danger; but he is deceived by the semblance of the thing, as children, or timid and ignorant men are. Then a word from his master re-assures him; if he has one, in whom he has confidence.

Consider, also, the emotion of anger. It is manifested in animals, under the same conditions, as in man. Take from a man, by force, that which he desires to keep, and he is angry,—so is a dog. The emotion of fear may be brought in to control the natural effects of anger, in animals as well as in men. Anger has the same effect upon the nervous and muscular systems of each. The eyes glare, the muscles become tense; there is an eagerness to fight,—to injure the aggressor,—and there seems to be an insensibility to suffering, from wounds and bruises. The tone of voice, in both men and animals, is changed by anger; and the change in both cases produces the same quality of voice. The emotion of anger is, then, we may fairly infer, alike in both,—in its cause, and in its effect on the motions of the body, its position, the voice and the act.

If we consider the emotions of joy, grief and shame, we shall find the similarity to hold. In the dog, at least, the animal most easily studied, we find them all manifested for like causes, and by like motions of eye, head, limb and tone of voice, as in man. A guilty dog drops the head and cannot look his master in the eye,—he manifests a sense of shame, when he is blamed, so that he thinks his master judges him guilty, or worthy of punishment. He watches the eye and voice of his master, for the first indication of returning favor, and expresses his delight as plainly as actions alone can express an emotion. These higher animals even know how to interpret the motions and tones of voice, that indicate some of these emotions in men, when they themselves are not directly concerned.

In the appetites and simple emotions, we can, then, make no distinction, in kind, between an animal and a man. The more closely we press the examination, the more marked does the likeness appear.

When we come to consider those instinctive impulses called desires, as desire of life, of property, of knowledge, of esteem and of power, the examination becomes more difficult. The animal seems to fear a death, of which he could have no knowledge ; and he fights for his own property, if it is only a bone. He curiously tries to investigate the nature of new objects, and unaccustomed sounds, if they do not arouse his fear, so as to overcome his curiosity. But all these actions are so constant, and so essential to his well-being, that we might expect they would be manifested by each animal of the higher types, as a necessary condition of life. In their operation, there is but little that simulates love of life, love of property, and love of knowledge in man; the difference, however, seems to be in the degree, or extent of these desires. But the desire of esteem is as well marked in animals as in man. Words of approbation seem as grateful to one as to the other; and both plainly do acts for the sake of the praise, and then come to seek their reward.

The desire of power is as well marked, but may perhaps be referred to those characteristics, which are essential to the animal's well-being, so that it is very difficult to point out its likeness to the desire of power in man. When strange dogs, or cattle, come together, the first thing that is to be settled, if they are near the same size, is, which is the better dog or ox of the two, with teeth or horns? If the weaker one plainly gives up, the larger will, sometimes, be satisfied with his acknowledged superiority. But generally, there must be a battle. When two men come together, it is the same, whether in the ring, in the senate chamber, or in the parlor. They measure each other's strength, and there is a constant struggle till one yields. Among animals, and men of muscle, the battle can be seen; but, in many cases, among men, the battle is only known to the two combatants.

It is generally said of man, that he has the desire for society. Society is so essential to his highest development, that it has been called a condition of his being, rather than a desire. But probably there is to man an enjoyment in society which is ultimate. He is a social being,—society is desired for its own sake. The same thing is true, also among animals. Horses, cattle, sheep and dogs, appear to seek each other's company, not only for the sake of defence, but simply for the sake of company. It may be said that dogs seek each other's company, by a remnant of the old, wolf instinct, that led them to hunt in packs. But this theory will not account for their play and gambols together, after they become acquainted. Nor will it account for the social nature of such herb-eating animals and seed-eating birds, as never hunted in company and never attempt defence in concert.

There is love of company, in one animal, as manifested for another of the same kind, and also for men, and for animals of different kinds, after the emotion of fear is overcome.

Shall we deny to animals an Æsthetic nature? Here, most of all, we need language to aid us. Let us be sure of our facts, and accept them as a basis for sound inference, instead of trying to explain them away under the influence of some favorite theory.

To the sound of music, most of the higher animals seem attentive. They mark differences of sound, that often escape the notice of many men. The dog will distinguish the sound of his master's sleigh-bell, as soon as its tinkle can be heard. The horse keeps step to the music, and learns to obey the bugle note. Singing birds accompany musical instruments, and imitate their sound, and the songs of other birds, to perfection. From this power of accurately discerning sound and the accompanying actions, we have fair ground for inferring that many of the higher animals not only distinguish musical sounds, but enjoy them. That wealth of melody, which fills our fields and groves, is sweet to the ear of man; but the songsters do not wait his coming, to begin their concert.

> "Is it for thee, the linnet pours his throat?
> Loves of his own, and raptures, swell the note."

That animals are sensible of beauty of form and color, it would be difficult to prove. It is, certainly, some argument in its favor, that they are most beautiful, in form and color, when they choose their mates. That they admire the landscape, over which they wander, or gaze from the giddy Alps, with the emotion of awe, or wonder at their sublimity, is something which we can never know. These high emotions can be revealed only by the face and tongue of man. But it is sometimes said that all this enjoyment, which comes to animals through the senses, arises from a low form of activity which betokens no intelligence or thought. Do animals reason? After eliminating all instinctive acts, which simulate the rational acts of men, do we find that animals perform any acts, by the same powers, and in the same manner, as men do, under the guidance of Intelligence? If they do not, then we must acknowledge that there is introduced into the works of nature, a false show, which is utterly abhorrent to our notions of truthfulness, and subversive of confidence in all our reasoning from natural phenomena. Animals, certainly, learn by experience, and often guide their lives as wisely by it, as most men do. Birds fear hawks instinctively; but they learn, by experience, that man and many other things are to be dreaded, and the conditions under which they are most dangerous. The crow learns that men walking alone, are apt to be dangerous; and that when riding, they are comparatively harmless. He soon allows the train of cars to thunder by him, while he sits by the road side, as unmoved by its roar, and fire, and smoke, and engineers, as he is by the clouds that pass over him. He has learned that locomotives, and the men on them, are not dangerous to crows.

The elephant, that has broken through a bridge, fears to trust himself upon another, until he has satisfied himself that it is safe. Old animals learn to fear dangerous things, which young animals may be destroyed by, and to disregard other things, that frighten the young. There is, in this respect, a very wide range of experience for many animals. The same kinds of animals vary in their knowledge, according to their age and opportunity of learning, as men do.

Probably there is no such thing as stupidity in Instinct proper. It is a difficult question to settle; but we judge so, on account of the great uniformity in the work of those animals, like bees and silk-worms, the work of which must be entirely instinctive. Natural selection would secure uniformity, within certain limits; and there probably is, as we have before suggested, the same sort of variation of Instinct, in the same species, as there is of organic structure; but so far as we can judge, the difference, in the work of insects of the same kind, seems to arise from some disease or trouble with the functions of the body; and not with the Instinct, as a guiding power.

But there certainly are intelligent, and stupid animals,—animals without experience, and those with an experience, which they turn to good account. Horses and dogs differ almost as much, in their ability to learn from their own experience, or to be taught by their masters, as men do.

But, it is said by some, that this apparent learning, from experience and observation, is only a low form of association of remembered sensations and is never connected with real *thinking*. As an assertion, this statement can have but little weight; and, as a proposition, we have yet to see it sustained by any satisfactory proof. We see the same effects in animals, which we know come from thinking in us, —we see that certain acts of theirs are the same as we perform, and we find the conditions so entirely the same in both cases, that we feel called upon, in all honesty, to infer thinking in the animal, until we can find an argument against it better than those that consist in denial, or which start from premises that beg the whole question.

The whole process of taming and training animals depends upon the fact that they learn by experience. When a wild squirrel is first caught, he trembles with fear, and his heart throbs, as your own would, at the roar of a lion in the jungle, or the war-whoop of the savage close at hand. He defends himself instinctively, with all his power, and with the weapons nature has given him. Now put him in a cage, and daily feed him, and treat him kindly, if that is possible while he is caged. By degrees, he trusts you more and more, until he is tame, and trusts you implicitly. His instincts are not changed. He still fears what he considers dangerous; but he has learned, by experience, that you are not dangerous, though he once judged you to be so.

The whole art of trapping animals consists in deceiving their judgment. This judgment is to a certain degree, instinctive, as we have shown; but it certainly is not entirely so, in the case of the higher animals. They become cunning as they are hunted. No animal knows instinctively, that iron is dangerous; as may be readily proved. Rats will run over all sorts of iron utensils, until one is caught in a trap; and after that, his fellows generally give that particular piece of iron-mongery, a wide berth. If it persistently remains at the rat-hole, and snaps up a few, which have not learned the danger, that hole will be deserted, as a dangerous place for rats.

A fox learns that a trap is dangerous only when it is set; and, sometimes, the trapper has to match his wit against that of the fox, and often finds himself outwitted in the end. The fox will dig out his trap and spring it, and then take all the bait. Such old fellows have been caught by turning the trap upside down, so that the fox was evidently caught, as he dug under the trap, to spring it. When an animal thus gives a trapper extra trouble, he knows well before it is caught, that it is an old one,—one which, in addition to the instinctive cunning and knowledge common to the species, as their necessary outfit in life, has a good fund of experience gained, as men gain theirs, by hardships and dangers.

There is one fact connected with the fear of enemies among animals, that is worthy of attention, though we do not feel sure, at all, that we have any satisfactory explanation for it.

That individual animals should become wild, by being hunted, is easily accounted for; but all the animals of a particular district soon become wild after men begin to hunt there. The character of the whole species, in that place, seems to be changed. This is observed to be true, even, of fishes. When the western counties of Massachusetts were first settled, the trout were easily taken in the streams; but now their whole character seems to be changed, to a degree very difficult to be accounted for, on the theory of individual experience; so that we are driven to the conclusion, either that there is a method of communication among these low animals, or that the timidity of the parent, acquired from danger, and a particular form of danger, is very readily transmitted to the young. This latter explanation seems the most plausible: and it will probably be found that those low animals, to which is denied the power of transmitting knowledge to their descendants, by tradition, have given to them a physical susceptibility, so that the benefits of experience are transmitted to the young, in regard to those things needful for the preservation of the species. This would be in harmony with the general plan of creation, as manifested in other provisions for the preservation of the species, by the plasticity of their nature; and it accounts for the observed facts in domestication, and among the wild animals. One has only to visit the coast of Iceland, where the Eider-ducks are protected by the inhabitants, and the coast of Greenland, where these birds are hunted by the Esquimaux, to see the marked difference in their habits, in the two places. In Iceland, they are almost as tame as domestic fowls; while in those parts of Greenland, where they have been hunted, they are among the most wary of birds. We simply call attention to the subject, and leave it for future observers to give us sufficient data for determining, with certainty, the true cause of that sudden change in all the animals of a region, after a new form of danger appears among them.

If animals learn by experience, this fact alone would settle the question of memory. But facts are abundant showing that animals remember faces even, and that for years. They often remember what happens but once; nor does this process of memory seem to be a mere bald association of ideas, connecting persons and places with pleasure and pain, only when those persons or places are again perceived by the senses. There are some facts which seem to show that there is, in the animal, a sphere in which mental reproduction is as independent of sensible objects, and as perfect, as in man. The hound, that has been hunting, often dreams of the chase. His limbs move, and he barks and pants for breath, in his eagerness. If now he is suddenly awaked, it is amusing to see him rapidly glance around him, as though looking to see where the game has vanished. After, apparently, satisfying himself that it was only a dream, he settles back, for a second sleep, with all the gravity of a man.

From all these facts, we infer that through the senses, men and the higher animals have the same kind of sensations,—that pleasure and pain are brought to both, through the nervous system, under similar conditions. That they have the same kind of emotions, is inferred, because the same manifestations through the physical system, that indicate fear, joy, anger, and shame in us, are seen in them, under just such circumstances, as would call forth those emotions in man.

In a word, then, the appetites and desires, so far as we can trace them, in men and animals are alike. Animals remember places, persons, and events. They love and hate. Harsh words and blows repel them, and often render them vicious. Kind words and good treatment will secure their confidence, good service, and affection. They learn much from their own experience; and, especially, they are able to come into such relations to man, as to comprehend his desires and perform his commands.

All these operations certainly involve thinking, as we have defined the word, and as it is generally used. If we accept some different definition,—one that eliminates all these elements, or which introduces such elements as cannot be indicated by any of these manifestations, of which dumb animals are capable, let us know just what this definition is. When we have the definition, it will be for the one giving it to show, by something more than mere assertion, that animals are excluded, even according to his own definition, from the list of thinking beings.

What then, in the animal, is the governing principle? We say, INSTINCT, or the spontaneous, self-directing activities, in distinction from free Intelligence, a degree of which animals possess. This we attempted briefly to show in the last lecture; and shall more fully illustrate, when treating of man. But at this point of the discussion we wish to say, that while we concede Intelligence to the higher animals, in distinction from Instinct, we find nothing in them that can control Instinct, or any power by which the animal may be said to control its own destiny. One instinct may, from certain circumstances, control another; as when parental love overcomes the fear of danger; but when we consider the acts of animals, as a whole, we find them so completely under the dominion of the instinctive principles, that the results are almost precisely the same, in all the thousands of a given species. It is this control of Instinct, making Intelligence a *servant*, rather than accepting it as a *master*, which gives the uniform plane to the life of animals, of the same species, when left to themselves. This control of Instinct, as being the leading power in the animal, is so apparent, that it probably accounts for much of the reluctance, on the part of many, to recognize Intelligence in animals at all. It is natural to think of Intelligence, wherever it is present, as ruling Instinct; because it thus rules in man. But because Intelligence in animals, takes its place as a servant, under the control of Instinct, it has, in many cases, been entirely overlooked, or its existence denied. It has been taken for granted, that Intelligence must rule, wherever it is present. In water, there is cohesion sufficient to form a liquid, but gravitation rules; and the current of water moves on as this force determines. Cohesion plays a subordinate part, and only enables gravitation to give the water greater power, as it moves. When cohesion increases, by the fall of temperature, gravitation still acts upon the particles, but it no longer controls their movements. The icicle holds firmly in its place, the frozen river refuses to flow, and crystals of ice shoot upward, in mockery of gravitation. In water, cohesion is the servant of gravitation; in ice, it becomes its master, though it can never escape wholly from its power. So, Intelligence in the animal, like cohesion in water, must bend all its energies in obedience to the instinctive principles, which control the actions of animals, as gravitation does the particles of water. But in man, Intelligence has become like cohesion, in ice and in the solid rock, which keeps them in form, and gives strength to the iron, and beauty of form to the crystal, in spite of gravitation, though they never escape wholly from its power.

From this capacity of animals for suffering and enjoyment, we infer that they have rights, though this is denied, on technical ground, as their power of thinking has been denied.

Animals have the right to get all the good out of life they can, in subordination to the higher beings placed over them. It is said animals have no conception of such rights, and therefore cannot have them. That they have no such conception remains to be proved; but in the mean time, we appeal to the sense of kindness implanted in their masters, till that is blunted by brutality, or a philosophy that has little to recommend it.

An invasion of their right to enjoyment, they instinctively repel. And the natural feelings of men, cry out against any wanton infliction of pain upon dumb animals. Those who torment them, are always cruel to men. The laws justly protect them against cruel masters; and in these laws, the community recognizes the rights of animals. Such laws ought to be better enforced than they are. The bodily suffering of animals may not be as keen, as that of a man,—if it were, they could hardly endure, as long as they do, all the cruelties practised upon them, through thoughtlessness, pride, anger and avarice.

It is difficult to prove that there is, in the animal, any sense of injustice, though there are manifestations that look as though there might be. In some cases, the punishment they inflict, is not for defence, but, plainly, on account of some long remembered abuse. But so helpless are animals, against the cruel wrongs practised upon them, that their sufferings, for the moment, make every honest man indignant, almost every time he passes through the streets. One would be glad to believe that animals are spared suffering from a sense of injustice —that keenest pang which man is called upon to endure.

LECTURE IX.

INSTINCT IN MAN GROWING OUT OF HIS APPETITES.—ANIMAL IN THEIR ORIGIN.

Man and Animals compared.—Observation and study a necessity for Man.—The higher Ruling Principle.—Free Personality.—Complexity of Man's Nature.—Origin and use of the Appetites.—Narrow range of Animal Instinct in the child.—Nursing.—Fear.—Moral Instincts.—Animal Instincts to be governed.—Marriage.—The desires.—Desire of Life, of Knowledge, of Power, of Esteem, of Society.—Revolutions and Reformations.—Summation of Activities.

MAN is called a rational being, in distinction from the brutes. He is certainly entitled to this distinction, as a being in whom Reason ought to control all the activities. Has he Instinct,—the same in kind as we have found among the lower animals? We have attempted to show that animals have Intelligence; but Intelligence subordinated to their Instinct, which always controls, so that almost uniform results are secured, among animals of the same species, when left to themselves. It has so long been taken for granted, by a large class of writers, that animals possess nothing but Instinct, to account for their actions, that the assertion, that they possess Intelligence, shocks many, as an attempt to break down the distinction between man and brutes.

And the assertion, which we now make, that man has a wider range of Instinct than any other animal on the globe, may be regarded as another attempt to break down the distinction, upon which we pride ourselves. We make no attempt to break down distinctions. We wish to find them, where nature has placed them,—as we mark distinctions in a natural classification,—and not to invent distinctions, or make them where they only seem to exist, on account of some accidental characteristic, as is done in artificial systems of classification.

If man has, in him, something higher than an animal, it does not destroy his animal nature; but it is something added to that nature. This animal nature of man, we are first to consider; for it is an essential part of us, while we remain in this world. We have already shown that the bodies of the higher animals are essentially the same as those of men. The bones, and muscles, and nerves, in both correspond; modified only according to the habits of each. We are of the earth, as well as they. We have no element, in our bodies, not found in theirs. Our bodies are subject to the same laws as theirs, in every respect, except as they have given to them certain changes of activities, to fit them for special modes of life, as in the case of hibernation. We find in ourselves, no new law of physiology. Every effort costs the waste of tissue, in the ox which turns the furrow, and in the husbandman, who holds the plough. Hunger, thirst, weariness and sleep come to both alike. That the human body is all animal, there can be no doubt. And, as an animal, man has precisely the same instincts, in kind, as other animals; and to the number and degree, that he needs them, according to the same principle, which we have found to prevail among the lower animals. We have found Instinct to be simply a method of action, involving impulse to perform the act, and knowledge and skill enough, without experience, to supplement a parent's care. We have found that nature gives just as little Instinct as possible everywhere; and leaves as much to experience as possible, without endangering the loss of the species. If she gives more instinctive knowledge to the young of any kind, it is because she gives less to the parent; giving most of all to those young, which never know a parent's care. Now, applying these principles rigidly to man, as an animal, we should expect him to possess animal instincts, mainly as *impulses*. We should expect him to have little of instinctive knowledge or skill, because the parent is able to supply both, and has the natural affection, or instinctive love, to ensure the proper action, or the best action according to her judgment. She is guided mainly, by experience. Instinct never gives her perfect knowledge and skill, as it sometimes does the lower animals. The whole machinery of man's nature, is so arranged that observation and study have always been demanded, and always will be demanded. While the instincts of the child and parent commence in impulses, just as they do in all other animals, the knowledge and skill are left to be acquired. And this knowledge can be increased, from generation to generation. Here, then, in what, at first sight, might seem to be the imperfection of the animal instincts in man, we find the intimation of his high nature,—his capacity for improvement, and the necessity for it,—and also the intimation that Intelligence must guide him, even as an animal; for his instincts, which are mainly impulses, only lead or drive him to ruin, unless they are directed and controlled. Intelligence here must be the *master* of instinctive action, and not its servant, as among the lower animals.

It is in the supersensuous part of our being alone that we must look for something *different in kind*, from what we find in animals. That we shall find such a principle, we have no doubt; because we see in man results which mere animal powers show no tendency to reach. This principle is that, in man, which is highest in kind, and which ought to rule his whole being. It should be autocrat among the powers. It should, from its throne above in the higher nature, rule all below,—making Intellect itself an instrument,—as bodily instincts rule in the animal. The instincts of the animal grow out of his bodily organization—and, so far as the animal is concerned, they begin and end with that. The higher power in us, which should rule the body, sometimes demands of a man, that he rise above every animal instinct, and give up even life itself, although there may be none to admire or recount his deeds. He may be so true to himself, as to deliberately accept of death—die for the truth.

With every man, is the choice between the rule

of his higher, and lower nature. Though walled around by fate, or the laws of nature in the world without, and the laws of nature in his own structure and animal instincts, there is yet left to him, a throne of sovereignty,—which he may mount, if he choose,—from which, he declares what powers in him shall be servants, and which masters, for the time. He appoints the bounds of each, or he could not be a responsible being. Here we come to the mystery of *free personality.*

The instinctive powers of the higher nature, are ever present in man, and their agency is so intimately blended with the agency of the animal instincts, —sometimes wisely controlling them and sometimes basely yielding, while they run riot and defeat the very ends for which they were given,—that it is almost as impossible to separate the activities of the two natures in man, as to discern with the unaided eye, the yellow red and blue, that are woven together in the sunlight. We need a psychological prism, which shall completely untangle the web, and show the animal and the image of God, that together make up this complex being, man. In the animal, all is beautifully simple. Every impression, from without, awakens impulses which he may follow to the full demand of his nature, with profit either to himself or his species. His simple nature is self-poised. If harm comes to him, as an individual, it is in following an instinct, which he was made to follow, and which will, upon the whole, bring good to his race, when followed to its full demand. But every impression in man, that wakens the animal instincts, wakes with them, a watchful guardian, which was appointed to give them their bounds, and tell them when to act, and when to remain in quiet, though their strength may be that of Titans.

As we enumerate the animal instinctive principles in man, let it be understood then, that we regard them as constantly modified by a higher constitution, or principle of action, of which we shall in the future speak.

As we compared animals with men, to show that they have something of that Intelligence, which appears full-orbed in man, so now we must compare men with animals once more, to show that our life begins on the same plane with theirs. The frog and the fish both begin their lives as animals of the same kind. The young frog is, to all appearances, a fish; but there is in him, from the beginning, a principle of organization that will in the end, give him lungs, and enable him to live in the upper air; while the fish must continue to breath by gills, during his whole life. So man begins his life, to all outward appearances, as the lower animals begin theirs,—more helpless, indeed, because his helplessness is supplemented by the enduring love and care of the mother.

The occasion for most of the lower forms of activity, in animals and men, are the appetites, as we have shown. They arise as naturally, from the physiological condition of the body, as hair grows upon the head or nails upon the fingers. It is as difficult to account for the origin of one of these, as for that of the other, and no more so. There are connected with the body still other forms of impulse and guidance, that secure purely automatic, or reflex action. But in the appetites, we find the first provision for those constantly recurring activities, which lead to definite, voluntary action, and are plainly provided for the preservation of the individual and the species—so powerful in their demands, that they cannot be forgotten, nor be neglected without producing suffering and injury. When Appetite calls, Instinct answers by some *voluntary* act. The nature of that first instinctive act varies as much as the degree of perfection of organs, with which the animal comes into the world, and for the same reason. The bodily organs of the animal vary just in proportion to the ability of the mother to take care of him; and the same is true of his instincts. Each animal, from the lowest to man, has just enough of organization and of Instinct, to supplement the care which the mother is ready to bestow upon him; and this care of the mother, depends upon the structure and functions of her body and her instincts. Among the fishes, or most of them, no parent's care is needed. The organization and instincts of the young fish are sufficient to preserve life from the beginning. As soon as the material in the egg is consumed, from which the fish was hatched, he is ready to hunt food for himself. As the period arrives, when other instincts are needed, they appear, as the different parts of his body appeared in the egg, at the proper time.

Many insects come into their highest form, with organs and instincts perfect, from the first moment of that life. Birds that cannot fly, walk, or see when they are hatched, have mothers, which build nests, in anticipation of their coming, and have the instinct to bring them the food they need. The chickens and young partridges leave the nest at once, pick the food which the mother finds, and often find it for themselves. They gather under the wings of the mother for warmth, and sometimes for protection, but rush from her in such danger as she cannot protect them from.

The Opossum and all the marsupial tribe, have young more immature than other animals, but the mother has a pouch, in which they are securely carried. Their imperfect development, at birth, is just supplemented by this curious special structure in the parent. These are instances for illustration, but the result may be summed up thus: *The structure and Instinct of the young at birth, and the structure and Instinct of the mother combined, are just sufficient to give the young a fair chance in the world, so that the species may be preserved;—one of these elements supplements the other.* If the chances are still largely against the individual, so that the species would seem to be in danger, then the number of individuals from a single parent is increased.

The same law holds in general, in the human race. The child is one of the most helpless of all beings, as it commences life; and it is dependent upon the care of others much longer than any other animal with which we are acquainted. But its long years of helplessness are provided for in the natural love of parents, and the common feelings of humanity and considerations of the public good. These all become strengthened in man, just in proportion as he rises above the condition of an animal.

But what of the child's animal instincts? They are brought within the narrowest limits, but appear in regular order as he develops, as we have seen to be true of all other animals. At the demand of appetite, the child is as ready to nurse, as the young bird is to raise its head for food.—This, we consider a purely instinctive act. We know attempts have been made, by very high authorities,* to show that this act of the child is not instinctive, but simply a reflex action,—in the beginning, entirely involuntary. We cannot believe this, at all. But if it could be proved, it would only show that in the human species, a reflex action is provided for, which simulates and *takes the place* of Instinct, in the lower animals. If the act is not instinctive, it is certainly lower; as all reflex actions are lower than instinctive, and supplementary to them, in both animals and men.

As soon as the child can discern, it instinctively fears danger, before it can possibly have learned, by experience, that there is danger. It fears a stranger's face, and clings to its mother for protection, before it has any rational ground for fearing any one. It has, like an animal, instinctive dread of danger, but it has not yet learned what is dangerous. It needs a mother's care; but all her cautions in

* Maudsley, p. 63; and others.

childhood, would have little effect, were it not for this instinctive fear. This supplements her care, and instructions,—it is all that gives her warnings any weight, until later, the child's instinctive love for her, and love of approbation and reward, lend their aid; and finally, the high Instinct of his moral nature, of which "OUGHT" is the natural expression, is ready to take the helm. Henceforth his activities may be ruled by this higher nature, as the animal's are from his lower. He will make mistakes, even while that rules; but he can grow in knowledge evermore, while the animal, having knowledge sufficient to secure life, given to him without experience, can never make acquirements higher than his bodily instincts can use, in their narrow round.

—When, later in life, the son seeks a wife, and the daughter leaves her home, and goes forth to cast her lot, for life, with a comparative stranger, we see an exhibition of Instinct that is a marvel—one that often defies all the dictates and controlling power of boasted Reason. It is all very well and right to talk of sensible marriages; and of law, as regulating marriage; that is all right; because man is made to control his animal instincts—to bring one into subordination to another. And his instinct to form Society, and protect it, so as to secure the good of the whole, leads him, through the agency of his higher intellectual and moral nature, to prescribe certain rules by which individual instincts shall be governed. By prescribing rules for the animal instincts, and by punishing the unrestrained action of those instincts as a crime, man shows at once, that his governing power is higher in kind, than his animal nature. But if he is wise, he never attempts to entirely check an instinct, but he directs it into the right course and then favors it, to its full activity, in subordination to Reason. And the right course of the appetites and instincts in man, can only be learned by experience. And just in proportion as there is ability to learn by experience, is there chance for loss before the experience comes. Liability to suffering from ignorance, and ability to improve by experience, are as necessary polarities, in the same being, as capacity for suffering and enjoyment are necessary polarities. As much as one is diminished, so much is the other weakened; as by weakening the polarity of one end of a magnet, you weaken the other at the same time. As, in man, the ability to profit from experience is at its maximum, because he can avail himself of the experience of others in the past as well as present, so is the danger of loss from ignorance, in following the instincts which in him, are simply impulses, and never fully directive, as they are among the lower animals. They are powerful—must be heeded—but in general need instruction and law to direct them; both of which, to be of any value, must be simply the echo of experience. They never will be perfect, till they are the true echoes of the best possible experience.

So then marriage, high and holy as it is, around which all that is most lovely, and pure, and sacred on earth, centres, has its origin in the instinctive nature of the race—in the same instincts, that appear in all the higher animals, which even there are so beautiful that the philosopher is made to say,—

> "In parental care and nuptial love,
> I learn my duties from the dove."

Those who think the instincts of humanity are to be ignored, in the relation of the sexes, forget that man has an animal nature; and those who think the instincts are a sufficient guide, forget that he belongs to that noble class, who are permitted to learn, and to become wiser by new experience in every generation. They both shoot wide of the mark,—or, to use another figure, while they are looking at the same shield, they are gazing upon opposite sides; and while they thus stand, there is no chance for agreement as to all the devices and inscriptions which the shield bears.

The DESIRES are generally regarded as distinct from the Instincts. There is certainly no ground for this distinction, if we consider their method of action, and remember that some instincts involve impulse as well as guidance. Some of the desires have the same relation to the welfare of the being, as the appetites have; that is,—they are impulses to action—instinctive impulses—the foundation of both instinctive and intelligent acts. Their action is often complex, and often intertwined with the action of the acknowledged appetites and instincts. But the confusion has arisen, mainly, from regarding Instinct as a distinct thing, rather than as a certain method of action common to all classes of powers, in all beings with which we are acquainted, either as the sole condition of their life, or the first condition of their intelligent action. The desires are thought to belong to the mind, rather than to the body; and this is undoubtedly true of some of them, for they neither originate from any function of the body, nor have special reference to its welfare. It is their method of action, which we now consider, and not the plane or sphere of their activity. But then we find a certain similarity of action running through every plane of being. The tree must feed, digest and assimilate,—so must the body of man,—so must his mind,—so must his moral nature. There is a wonderful similarity running through the whole, in the substratum of each new plane; though something new may be added, as we go up from plane to plane. Man is made up of layers, like the geologic strata. As we come up through the formations of the earth, new forms of life appear, higher and better than those before; but they are cast according to the same types that we found below. There is unity of plan, though no necessary connection of actual relationship, of one form with the other. So man, in his unity, like the globe, appears in stratas,—vegetative life, animal life, intellectual life, moral life,—all proceeding with so much similarity of action, that it is not strange, these stages are considered by some, as simply different degrees of development of the lowest; as man himself is regarded by some, as the offspring of some lower animal.

The desire of life, which is sometimes placed above the instincts, as belonging to the mind, is certainly one of the lowest of the instincts, in the sense of being the broadest, and as being only an impulse. It gives rise to a whole series of definite instinctive acts among animals, and of rational acts, among men, which tend to preserve life. This is true, to some extent, of the remaining desires,—desire of knowledge, desire of power, of property, of esteem, and of society. These are the basis of the social nature of man. The last leads him to seek society, the others tend to regulate society,—are impulses and hints for experience to build upon. "Men," says Emerson,* "as naturally make a state, or a church, as caterpillars a web;" and this is true; because the impulses and the hints are in them. But while the caterpillars have, for themselves, one best form of web, which appears as regularly, with each new, uninstructed and inexperienced brood, as the number of rings in their bodies, or the color of the hairs and spots that cover them, man is left to work out the best form of state-web or church-web, for himself; by entangling himself and fellows, in all sorts of make-shifts, which may be a curse to him, or may be well enough, in one age or one part of the world, but perhaps are no more fitted for him as he grows, than the bark of the young sapling is fitted for the trunk of the full grown tree. The bark of the tree, and the web of both state and church, must

* "Conduct of Life," p. 176.

be rent and thrown off, while larger bark, and more enlightened forms of government, in state and church, take their place; unless they can all grow in time to save the rending. They must all yield to the demands of that expanding organism, which they were made to serve; be it the tree-trunk, or society. Revolutions and reformations are the rending of the old *exuviæ* of state and church, under the promptings of a higher life. This transition period, necessary for more perfect growth, is the most critical time for animals and men.

The first impulse then, to every voluntary act in man, that is necessary to preserve the life of the individual, the continuance of the species and the formation of society, seems to be as purely instinctive, as any act of an animal. But the impulse, to all these acts in man, must be limited, and, in most cases, directed in him, by some higher principle, which can act rightly only in the light of experience; while in the animal, Instinct not only gives the impulse, but is self-directive, and self-limiting, or is limited in its action by the vegetative functions of the body. The animal, in a state of nature, finds his highest perfection in going just as far as Instinct and function of organs will allow. Man, giving himself up to such influences, without the guidance and limitation, which his intellectual nature affords, and which his moral nature demands, sinks below the brutes, as a matter of course.

We have thus far used the word INSTINCT for

convenience, nearly in the sense given by Whately as a blind tendency to some mode of action independant of any consideration, on the part of the agent, of the end to which the action leads. This is as good a definition as any that has been given, but it does not cover the whole ground of instinctive action, as we have shown more than once, during the course of these lectures. It is well for us at this point, to enumerate all the powers or activities, which we have now found in the higher animals and man, which they have, to some degree, in common. It is in this way only, that we can point out the true nature and sphere of Instinct in both, and this we desire to do, whether we are able to give a single definition which will be satisfactory or not.

1. We find Physiological agencies, by which the body is built up and repaired, and provision made for the reproduction of the species. These agencies belong to the vegetative life of the animal and man; volition has no direct control in any of their operations. They supply the conditions for voluntary action.

2. We find a sensitive nature, by which the animal is brought into relations to the world, by sensation and sense—perception. This is the true animal nature.

3. We find certain reflex actions, the result of *stimuli* acting upon the vegetative and animal nature. They are involuntary movements required for the benefit of the body—as winking, coughing, sneezing, and the like.

4. We find the appetites, which arise from the functions of organs, but are powerful *stimuli* to action.

All these are conditions for voluntary activity; and upon these the instincts, including the desires, begin to appear,—and they involve several distinct things, as follows:

a.—*Impulse, arising beyond the sphere of the appetites,*—as the impulse to migrate and to store food for winter,—also the desires, so-called.

b.—*Knowledge without instruction or experience, for meeting the demands of the appetites and desires, and for doing all those things essential to the continuance of the race.*

c.—*Knowledge arising independently of the appetites,*—as recognition of certain enemies without instruction, or experience.

d.—*Skill without instruetion or practice,*—to carry out the plans necessary to meet the demands of the appetites and other impulses required for the existence of the species.

These three distinct things are involved in the manifestations of those activities, which are together labelled INSTINCT, *Impulse*, *knowledge* and *skill*, —they are all given, as needed to begin life,—as organs are given for the same purpose. These products of the animal's being determine nothing of his rank. They simply say, " *We are here, because this animal must live—we are here to meet the conditions of his life, till he has a chance for experience. If he is not to have that, we must go farther and do the whole work; and do it so that the wisest being on the globe cannot improve upon our work, though we work through* BEES *and* SPIDERS *and* WORMS—*the lowest forms that live.*

Next above the instincts, we have found Intelligence, which enables the actor to comprehend the probable results of his own acts before they are put forth. It may rise much higher than this, but here its work begins. All these activities and powers here enumerated, we find in man and in the highest of the lower animals. So far, certainly, the animals differ from each other, and from man, only in degree. But while all these activities take their rise in the animal nature, they shoot up higher in man, and so interweave themselves with every nobler power, that we shall find them constantly re-appearing, as we consider the higher nature of man. So intimately blended are the natural affections with the moral nature of man, that even the natural affections of animals, which give them a social nature, have been referred to by some, as proof of a moral nature in them. We hope to make plain the distinction between these two natures, before the close of these lectures.

LECTURE X.

RELATION OF THE INSTINCTIVE PRINCIPLES OF ACTION TO THE RATIONAL AND MORAL NATURE OF MAN.

Intuitions and Instincts.—Something must be given as a basis for Reasoning and for acting.—Agricultural Ants.—Belief in the uniformity of Natural phenomena, from observation.—Instinct acts in reference to contingent events.—Purposes for which Instinctive Principles are needed by man.—The Desires.—The Affections.—Love of Society.—Knowledge, Property, Power, Esteem.—Faith.—Benevolence.—Need of guidance in man.—The Ruling Power.—Conflict between the higher and lower Instincts.—The Comprehending Power.—Difference between man and the highest animals.— "OUGHT."—*Sense of obligation.*

THAT man would have animal instincts, as an impulse at least, we should expect, since his body has essentially the same structure, and the same relations to the world, as have the bodies of all the higher animals. It now comes in order for us to inquire, if there is Instinct, or any principle of action like Instinct, reaching into his rational nature; in virtue of which nature, he is wont to claim great superiority over the lower animals, and difference from them *in kind.* We are also called upon to trace more fully than we have done, the connection between the animal instincts and this higher nature of man, that we may learn how far they are modified by it, and to reach, if possible, that guiding and controlling power for all the activities, of which we have spoken.

It is generally conceded by Psychologists, that man, as a rational being, has certain intuitive notions in regard to being, quantity, causality and the like. It belongs to Mental and Moral Philosophy to treat of these notions fully. But we are here called upon to mark more clearly, than we have done, the difference between *Intuition* and another principle in the higher nature of man, which seems to be the same in its method of action as acknowledged Instinct. *Intuitions* belong to us as rational beings simply; *Instincts*, as beings called upon to act. We believe some things *instinctively*, and some things *intuitively*. The words have been often used interchangeably, though, in general, they have been so used as to show that there ought to be a difference between them. We will start with a distinction, which we trust our past and future discussions will, when taken together, show to be a just one.

INSTINCT belongs to beings, as *acting*, and so relates to the nature and possible combination of things, and the order of events. Our knowledge of these, and of our right relations to them, even in the highest realm, is secured partly by instinctive action; and necessarily so, because Instinct gives all that is necessary for action, which we cannot learn by observation and experience,—all that is necessary as a basis for experience, as well as the impulse to perform certain acts.

INTUITION, on the other hand, relates to abstract truth, to all that is necessary as a basis for correct reasoning, and for conducting the process,—whether in the field of pure intellect or morals. What we know *intuitively*, will always be true. What we know *instinctively*, is true only because this order of things is what it is. What we know intuitively, we cannot believe to be different from what it is,—it is in this sense, *necessary* truth. What we believe instinctively, might be different from what it is—it is *contingent.*

Instinct, then, has the same relation to action that Intuition has to thought, or the logical process. In all reasoning, something must be given as *known.* If this were not done, no reasoning would be possible. In acting, something must be given as an *impulse and as an initial directing power*, or knowledge from experience would be impossible,—there would, in our actions, be no relation to the universe in which we are placed.

The use of Instinct to animals and men, is to give them impulses to action, and guidance in spheres where the appetites, as functional, cannot reach, to start them in the right direction, and to add impulses on the way, at the same time giving such knowledge and skill as could not be gained by experience,—or perhaps better, to secure from them such action as could not otherwise be secured, without such an experience as would be destructive to such beings, and thus be constantly defeating the end for which they were made. We can best illustrate this principle by referring once more to examples in the animal kingdom already mentioned. The fowl has an instinctive fear of death, of which it knows nothing as yet. Fear is given to secure the requisite action, without experience, because the experience of death would be final,—there would be, after that, no chance left to profit by the experience. Therefore a fear is given to act instinctively, just as though the animal had learned all the terrors of death, by experience. Certain animals, also, are thrown upon the world without any parental protection. All such animals act, from the beginning, in securing food and caring for themselves, as though they had already learned many things by experience. The young Salmon wakes to life far up in the cold waters of the mountain streams, perhaps. There is no parent, and no fish of experience there to guide him, or from which he can learn. At least, if he learned from the fishes in the river at all, it would be to remain there. But when the proper time comes, all the thousands of young Salmon start for the sea as their appropriate home, although they have never seen it. They act exactly as though they had had experience of the provisions of the sea for their use; and it is necessary for their well-being that they should so act. So much of impulse and direction must be given to them, if the species is to exist at all. The fowl, also, has not only the generic fear of death, instinctively, which is common to all animals, but it has an instinctive fear of certain things which might produce death. The fowl, that has never seen a hawk, and can know nothing of his nature from experience, is convulsed with terror at the sight of him. This enemy is known instinctively, because it is so deadly an enemy that knowledge by experience would be impossible to the fowl; or, at least, destructive to the species. It is necessary for the preservation of the species, that a fowl should fear a hawk instinctively, as well as that it should fear death instinctively; and so it has the fear of both, as an original outfit.

The abstract notion of cause and effect, and of their necessary relation to each other, is *intuitive.* This notion is necessary for some of the highest processes of reasoning known to man, if, indeed, we could have any notion of such processes without the gift to us of this primary knowledge. But that belief in the uniformity of nature which influences action, is not intuitive—it is partly instinctive and partly from experience, in both man and animals. Instinctive knowledge or belief, as a basis of action, is given to both, just as far as it is needful for commencing the work which experience can complete, without involving the absurdity of destroying the species in gaining the experience. And therefore Instinct gives much more impulse and guidance in regard to nature, to animals, than it does to man, and much more to some species of animals than to others. Facts illustrative of this statement will occur to every observer; but it may not be amiss to discuss still farther the relation of instinctive knowledge to that learned from experience, in regard to operations in nature.

Belief in the connection of cause and effect is, as we have said, intuitive; and we can never tell with certainty, that an animal has such a notion. It is the general opinion that he has not. But he comes, at once, into a world that makes an impression upon his senses, and he acts instinctively as though he believed that there is something without him which causes the sensations. He believes instinctively in an external world, if we can judge any thing by his acts. But all that we are sure of is that his acts are correlated to the world.

Undoubtedly, it is true of man, that he has an instinctive belief in the uniformity of nature's laws. But the belief that any particular event, the rising of the sun, for instance, will continue to occur, as it has in nature, is an entirely different thing. Probably, in man, such belief always comes from experience. It may be given to an animal without experience, when it is needful for him, or rather, for the species. Men plant in spring, expecting a harvest in autumn. The harvest may fail, and a particular experience is needed in each new place, and with each new kind of seed, to learn the best time of planting, and the best methods of culture, to secure a crop. Probably the use of seed, by men, for planting, is entirely the result of observation. Give any man a new seed, and he may be unable to secure its germination even; or, if it germinates, it may fail to produce fruit, because he does not understand its nature. It is plain that man has no instinctive knowledge to guide him in securing a crop. In the only case known in which animals, the "*Agricultural Ants*" * of Texas, raise, as well as harvest, a crop, the entire process is so complex, and yet uniform in all places, that it seems wholly the work of Instinct, as does also the care of other species of Ants for their herds of *Aphides*.† The expectation that there will be rain or snow in their season, probably every one will believe to be founded on observation and experience. More persons would differ as to our belief in the uniform order of the seasons, and the stated return of day and night. But little thought will convince us that these are as truly contingent, as is the coming of rain and snow. The cycles are so great, that we do not note the irregularity of their return; but we see agencies at work that might change them all, and probably are changing them all. Our intuitive belief in the relation of cause and effect, remains; but we learn by experience alone, the results which the causes now acting in nature produce. What has been always uniform in our experience, we *expect* will continue so.

Now it is necessary for some animals, that they should act, not only as though they possessed this generic belief in causation, but that they should also act in reference to *contingent events*, of which they have had no experience. This is also a very important point in the argument. The Squirrel, that has never seen a winter, lays up food in autumn when, from its abundance everywhere, it would seem that

---

* "Homes Without Hands," (Wood), pp. 370–372.

† Kirby and Spence, 7th. Ed., pp. 335, 336.

he had least need of doing it. Something like this is seen in all the provisions the animal makes for the change of seasons, and in the provisions which Nature makes for him. Physiological action prepares his body with a warm coat, as winter approaches. And if his food must fail in winter, and it is of such a kind that he cannot store it up, then Nature brings upon him a sleep, which saves food, and lasts till her table is spread for him again, in spring time.

The physical systems of animals and their instincts then, do have relation to the periodicity of these common, contingent events in the order of nature. They are adjusted to the length of the year, and even to the angle of the ecliptic with the equator. Such a relation is necessary for the very existence of many animals.

There is no proof that Nature makes any special provision in man for the change of seasons. But she has given to his system a wonderful power of self-adjustment, in meeting changes of climate at all times, with great rapidity. Man was made to have continuous summer or winter, as he might choose, or part of each; and to learn, by experience, the kind and amount of clothing fitted for him. Mr. Wallace speaks of it as a strong argument against the theory that man originated from the lower animals, by natural selection, that no hair is ever found upon his back, where the longest and most vigorous hair is found upon the lower animals.*

* "Natural Selection," p. 345.

It is also true, that there is no more hair upon northern than upon southern races. As Nature makes no provision, in the system of man, for change of seasons, but leaves him entirely to experience as a guide, so, probably, she denies to him any prophetic instinct, such as she gives to certain animals, by which they provide for the winter, that they have never seen the like of.

We have now come to a point in the discussion, where we shall best be able to trace the instinctive principles in the whole nature of man, by enumerating the purposes for which these principles are needed by him. They will, on examination, we think, be found to be the necessary conditions:—

1. *For life*—that is, the continuance of the individual and the species.

2. *For progress, of the individual and race*—that is, as the basis or condition of experience.

3. *For benevolence*—including under this term all disinterested labor for individuals and for society, as a whole, from natural or moral impulses.

4. *For worship*—including all specific acts, that acknowledge God and duties towards Him, or relations to Him, distinct from all other relations.

The instinctive principles, which secure these purposes, may be simply conditions, or occasions of specific actions; or they may be self-directive and self-controlling in the performance of specific acts, as manifested in some animals; or they may be mainly impulsive and directive, but needing control and limitation in their action, by some higher principle, that uses them as servants. And some of them may serve more than one of these purposes.

The instincts of the animal, so far as they seem to relate to his own welfare, appear to be confined mainly, if not entirely, to the first class,—those that preserve life,—securing to him, of course, so much enjoyment as comes by the normal activity of his powers; which never secure progress through the agency of their possessor alone. There the animal stops; but these instincts of the first class, in man, are but the stepping-stone to a higher nature, to the very summit of which, like principles of action, seem to be needed, and to exist. Certain it is, that man has the power to throw down over these instincts, which he has in common with the brutes, so much of his higher nature, that they become dignified, lovely, and the source of happiness, reacting upon, and aiding all that is above them; or he may abandon these instincts to their own uncontrolled action, so that they shall work out a degradation impossible among the brutes.

We have spoken of the appetites as the first condition, of the exercise of those instincts, which tend to preserve life. There may be certain *reflexive acts* which have been mistaken for instinctive, but probably all will agree that a truly instinctive act involves volition in some stage of its history. Every voluntary act that aims at some relation with the external world, would seem to involve some notion of the existence of such a world. We regard this notion of the existence of an external world as given, as the instincts are,—the essential outfit of every man and of every animal in which there is truly voluntary action, seeking relations to the world. Not that we suppose that animals or infants ever enunciate this truth of the existence of an external world to themselves, or have any theories or ideas respecting it, except that the belief is always present, as an element in the impulse to every voluntary act seeking an end in the world without the actor. Belief in the uniformity of Nature's laws, that is, that gravitation, or cohesion, or a specific kind of matter, under the same conditions, will always produce the same results, we are inclined, also, to regard as an original gift.

It may be found that the idea of causality is all that is constant, and that the rest of this belief is partly instinctive and partly inductive, the proportion that is instinctive varying according to the imperative demands of the animal, as we have already seen is the case, in reference to those events in Nature that are contingent, depending upon the condition of the causes necessary to produce them. At least we are compelled to treat all men, and all animals that we desire to make useful to us, as though they had either instinctively, or as an induction, a belief both in the existence of an external world and also in the principle of causality, in all the operations of nature. So much for the conditions of all voluntary action from the lowest to the highest. Experience, as a guide, rests upon them and would be useless without them.

But such conditions of action are not impulses to action; and these we want. The Appetites we have, but they are not always broad enough for all the wants of the being, and therefore instinctive impulses are found, which have no direct connection with the Appetites, though they may work in the same direction with them, or supplement their work. And among these instinctive impulses, we reckon the *Desires*, so called. It has been well said by President HOPKINS that the desire of happiness is generic. It is interwoven with all other desires. It is, in this respect, like the desire of life, which involves the fear of death—though probably the desire of happiness, in man, is broader than the desire of life, even. The desire of life may be lost, but the desire for happiness cannot be. Perhaps however, that a strict analysis would show that the desire of life is only lost, so far as it is judged to be a condition of suffering, rather than of enjoyment. And that the prospect of happiness, through life, must be lost, before life can be given up, without some higher purpose than the suicide has. The desire of life and the desire of happiness are the two great under-lying instincts into which all others seem to strike; or rather, all other instincts are the special methods of securing the demands of these, to the individual or the species. The relations to life and happiness, of the things instinctively aimed at by any being, are by no means always perceived by that being. This we have illustrated by many examples during this discussion, showing it to be an essential characteristic of an instinct, that it shall act promptly, and as though directed by Intelligence, where the good of the being absolutely demands it, though the being, in which it acts, even man himself, may be as ignorant of any reason for its acting, as he is of any reason for sleep or hunger, except that they come in consequence of a certain constitution that he has, he knows not how.

Of the instincts which belong to the first class, that have the Appetites as their basis, which are common to animals and men, we have already treated very fully, so far as they act by themselves.

We propose here only to call attention to the peculiar action of these instincts in the human species, as needing direction and limitation, from some principle distinct from themselves, and higher. The appetite for food is given to man, as to all other animals; but the choice of food, its production, preservation and preparation, are, with man, things to be learned by observation and experiment. Here he stands upon entirely different ground from any of the lower animals. Great advances have been made within a century, in our ability to properly administer to the demands of the appetite for food. Millions of acres of our domain, have been devoted to these experiments, and we have but just begun to learn what is best for men to eat, to meet the demands that are made upon them, and to ward off the diseases to which they are exposed. While man lives like an animal, this is a simple matter; but under a high civilization, it is complex and demands for its treatment, powers entirely different from any thing that we can call instinctive. And civilization is the true state of man, so that the appetite for food, which, in the animal, will take care of itself,—in man, becomes the occasion of study, of experiment, and of discussion. It not only aids in building up the body, but it calls upon the mind for counsel, as to how it may best perform its work.

In all that relates to the sexes, we recognize strong impulses from Appetite and Instinct, but in every direction see the need of control and restraint from some power entirely distinct from the appetite, or the instincts connected with it.

To say nothing of the mistakes of marriage, where even Reason and Pride are not strong enough to prevent wretchedness, we often see the instinctive love of parents ruining their children, in its blind efforts to secure their good. Conjugal, parental, and filial affections are as purely instinctive in men as in the brutes, and belong primarily to the animal nature—have their first impulses from that. But in man, they may be the source of suffering and degradation, defeating the end for which they were given, or they may extend much farther than it is possible for them to, among animals, and be lifted up into a sphere of beauty and permanence, unknown to animal life; mingling with all the instincts and powers of that higher nature, by which they must be controlled, if at all.

Husbands and wives, parents and children! We have but to look abroad in the world to see that the relations which these words suggest, produce the greatest blessings and the greatest sufferings which this world knows,—and that all the suffering, which we most deplore, comes from ignorance and want of control of those appetites, passions, and impulses which in animals are self-directive, but in man must be put under restraint and guidance from something entirely beyond their own sphere.

We hear much about civil laws as regulating these matters. And here we see the need of it; because these instincts are not self-regulative in man. They are to be governed by Reason and Conscience; and because these are too weak in many individuals, there must be law, which is the expression of the public reason and conscience, called into requisition to secure the best interests of all. And the only hope for proper laws, is in an enlightened conscience in the majority.

But to untangle this snarl of the past generations, will require much time and patience; and we fear it will not be made straight till much more mischief has been done, and men learn from a long, sad experience, what the true bounds of these instinctive principles in man are, and have wisdom and moral strength to give these principles that guidance and limitation, which they have no power to give themselves.

Distinct from the instincts, that secure the family relation, we have also considered the desire for society, which may be called an instinct. It is to some extent ultimate in its action, as securing enjoyment to men and animals, in virtue of their very constitution. But in man, this desire secures the conditions for the operation of those instincts of the second class, by which the progress of the race is mainly secured. Society is, certainly, a necessary condition for the exercise of some of the instincts of this class, as will be readily seen, when they are mentioned.

Prominent among the desires which belong to this second class, that secure progress, are the desire of knowledge, the desire of property, of power and of esteem. The desire of knowledge, of property, and of power, in a certain degree, may be necessary for securing life, or the best conditions of living. But in man, the impulse in each of these desires, certainly, goes beyond what the preservation of life demands; and plainly points to progress of the individual and the race, as its final cause. That desire of knowledge which leads to study and investigation for its own sake, prepares the way by years and ages of toil, observation and experiment, for those grand discoveries in science and practical applications of science, that now make the globe and all its forces, the servant of man. The steamboats, telegraphs, and other marvels of our age, come to us as the fruit of study, that had no promise of reward when the work was done. Love of knowledge led men in the past, and is still leading them, where there is no prospect of gain. But on the other hand, the desire of property obeyed in other individuals, has given that accumulation of capital which makes these grand enterprises of our day possible. Love of esteem in man, seems mainly for the benefit of society in securing from each one, those acts towards society and each member of it, which shall be best for both. These desires differ greatly in their strength, as a whole, or in their comparative strength, even in members of the same family. They may be strengthened by exercise, but are never weakened by it. One of them may be brought to the aid of the other, or be made subservient to it, as when knowledge is sought for the sake of the power it will give; or knowledge, property, and power are all sought for the sake of the esteem they will secure. Either of these instincts may become the master, and all the others ready servants; but the one that is master has no power of rightly controlling or limiting its own action even. *The controlling and limiting power is still beyond.*

Very different in its action from the Desires, but standing high, as an instinctive principle of progress, is *Faith*, or confidence in persons. It may be shaken, or directed in its action by experience, but it does not come from experience. So strong is it, that no amount of suffering from lying and deceit, will destroy a man's trust in the words of all his fellow-men. It is natural for him to believe them, and to trust them, as soon as the time comes when it is necessary that he should trust them. In childhood the trust is mainly centred on the parent, or the one in the parent's place, as it is best for the welfare of the child it should be.

Although we may say, in our haste, that all men are liars, we naturally trust men, till we have been often deceived; and then we distrust them only when we think they have some motive for deceiving us.

We find also another principle of action that secures progress, though the impulse to the action, in some cases at least, seems to be Benevolence,—the object of which is to secure happiness. We refer to the disposition of men to do what they can for the generations that are to come after them, without any reference to direct relationship. We are disposed to think the impulse is an instinctive one, which becomes strengthened and directed by specific, benevolent, social instincts. All such action is so opposed to selfishness that we must look to see it constantly repressed, and warped from its free exercise. Its existence, as a distinct principle, may be doubted; for the instinct, if it be one, is complex in its action, and in many cases, may be so intertwined with, or obscured by, the action of other instincts, as to be lost sight of.

Man desires to be remembered; and it may be said this desire leads him to do what shall be beneficial to the coming generations. Undoubtedly this is so, but in addition to this mode of gratifying the love of esteem, there is, probably, an instinct that leads him to do work for those whom he has never seen, and who will never hear of his name. "The old man plants trees, the fruit of which he never expects to pluck." And he does this without any necessary relation to family connections, though these may come in with their influences, to strengthen and direct this impulse.

We recognize this principle in our building, and public enterprises, and in our laws, which secure property for generations, and make permanent corporations.

This instinct might be reckoned as belonging to the third class, which are benevolent in their action, as we have already intimated, as well as to the second; for the division we have made cannot be sharply defined, as many of the desires and principles of action have several relations; and any one of them can be made the servant of another, as has been shown. But among the instinctive principles, which are strictly benevolent, are *pity* and *mercy*.

In our investigations thus far, we have found, in animals, all that they need for working out the best results, which it seems possible for such beings to reach. They have *impulse*, *guidance*, and *limitation* of *action* secured in the very nature of their appetites and instincts. Each one of these is so far self-regulative, as to make it best for the individual or the species, that it shall have activity uncontrolled by any power beyond its own sphere. The best condition which we can conceive of for an animal, when free from the disturbing influences of domestication, is to let him have an abundance of every thing needful to him, and then let him have entire liberty to follow every impulse.

Not so with man. We have found in him strong impulses,—impulses and instinctive principles of action of as wide a range as any animal has,—and more still remain to be considered. We find, as yet, nothing to direct and limit these impulses, to secure the highest good of man. We can hardly think of a worse condition for man, than to supply him with every thing needful for him, and then for him to give himself up, as animals may, to every impulse. The voice of the whole thinking world is, that there must be in man a power of self-control,—something outside of these activities, of which we have been speaking,—something that experiments with them, observes their action and determines their proper sphere of action, allowing one to act, and keeping another in abeyance, in spite of its clamors; in fact, ruling them, and making them its servants. This higher power seeks for, and determines the *Law of Limitation*, so fully explained by President HOPKINS. This law is, *that every power in man must be used so far, and only so far, as it is a condition of activity for the next higher power.* This limit of action for each power, the man must himself determine. And when that has once been determined, the *high, ruling power* within him, confines each of these servants to its own place, and exacts of it the labor required for the good of the whole.—It may learn much from these servants skilled in their own departments of labor, but it never should lose control of them. In that man, where this ruler is well informed, and uses the power which rightfully belongs to him, there is the order, harmony, happiness and progress of a well-ordered kingdom. But where the ruler is misled by ignorance, or fails through weakness or negligence, to control his subordinates, there is riot, waste, rebellion and ruin.

We speak of this *higher nature,* which rules in man as *one,* and so it is one, as something added to the animal nature; *but it involves distinct methods of activity,* which our present purpose does not require us to fully analyze. We shall only speak of this higher nature in man as ruling the lower activities, and trace instinctive impulses into it, and beyond it, into the strictly religious nature; in both of which, these principles appear abundantly, thus giving a whole field of instinctive activities in man, which either never exist in the lower animals; or, if they exist in them, they are beyond our power of discovery.

The instincts of the higher and lower nature of man are in constant conflict, because the lower are not limited, but are constantly pushing beyond their proper bounds, as they never do in animals. If the higher gain the day, man is worthy of the place he was made to fill, as the image of God and ruler of the globe,—having dominion over all its creatures, and over his own animal nature. But if the animal instincts take the control, there is no limit to his possible degradation.

The animal powers of man must be governed, then, because they are not self-regulative. They must be limited, and directed in their action, by some power or set of powers above them. This power the man has; or more strictly, he has a combination of powers, which makes him a ruler of himself, through the sovereign act of a free personality. The very fact that his lower propensities,—the *Appetites* and *Instincts*,—are not self-regulative, as in animals, but are capable of terrific power, even destructive power, when left to themselves, shows them to be admirably adapted for service. No matter how powerful any agency is, if it be directed and controlled. The more powerful it is the better. Steam, and gunpowder, and gravitation are powerful. How destructive they are in their uncontrolled action! How they crush and rend and kill! But the steam, when controlled, bridges the ocean, brings distant cities together, and, in the workshop, does the labor of millions of men. Gunpowder levels the mountains, and opens the riches of the mines. Gravitation crowds the waters through the wheel, and gives us a power that needs no fire nor fuel for its continued strength. What these powerful agencies are as servants, when controlled and directed by bands of iron, the animal instincts are when under control of that power in man, appointed to give them law. What, now, are the powers which this ruling principle in man must have, or rather, that the man must have, in order to rule himself? We will not attempt an enumeration of them singly, for that would carry us on to the ground of the Mental and Moral Philosopher, where contests are always raging in regard to definitions and the classification of the powers. We shall speak of these powers, singly or in groups, according to their office in this governing work.

And first of all, as a means of rightly performing this work, there must be *Comprehension.* The man must, by some power or set of powers, be as capable of understanding all his own powers, from the lowest to the highest, in their capabilities, and uses, as he is of comprehending any thing in the world without him, upon which he can experiment to advantage.

This comprehending power must, also, be able to give to the man an understanding of his relations to the world,—to make him a progressive being, this power must furnish the means of constantly adding to his knowledge—of widening its own sphere, and improving its own action.

The full comprehension of all the powers, activities and impulses, and of the relations of the man possessing these to the world, is the highest intellectual act possible, so far as the well-being of the man himself, in this world, is concerned. It is a thing so seldom done, that it is no wonder that, "KNOW THYSELF," should, for so many ages, have been considered one of the wisest of all sayings; and that the practice of the precept, should be considered wisdom itself. This precept has, perhaps, never been perfectly obeyed, either in the knowing of one's self or in the action, which seems to be necessarily implied, as the result of knowing. And as society becomes more complex in its organization, and the relations of every man become more widely extended, this knowledge of self as related to the world, becomes more difficult. Perhaps the difficulty of the problem increases as fast as the means are provided to aid in its solution. It can only be approximately solved, at mature age, and after careful education, for its solution requires trained powers and knowledge acquired by the experience and observation of ourselves and others. On this account, it is a natural thing for man to remain under parental control, till this condition of acting is reached. Nothing but a felt necessity for this, would justify the long minority of young men. They must be controlled by others, and be furnished with knowledge by experience, and observation and instruction, because they have neither sufficient knowledge nor self-control, instinctively, as animals have, to enable them to reach the best results, when left to follow every natural impulse.

This power of comprehension is generally exercised in a very imperfect manner, in the act of establishing those relations with the world, which naturally determine the direction of a man's activities for life. Even under the best conditions of society, the impulses are often followed blindly for awhile; and then comprehension comes in, and finding the work well begun, completes it,—or, finding it wrongly commenced, abandons it and begins anew; or makes the best of a bad case, too far gone to be rectified. In other cases, it never does its appropriate work; and the man floats through the world like a stick of drift-timber. In other cases still, where there is clear comprehension of relations and powers, and of desirable results, there seems to be too little ability to restrain or control the lower powers, and make them servants;

and the man is driven in this direction or in that according to the subordinate impulse that has usurped supreme power. The man is made a curse to the world, and a ruin, by being under the control of some appetite or instinct, which he knows he ought to control, or which the common judgment of the world declares he ought. We begin at this point to see what a wide difference there is between man,—when we consider his whole nature,—and the highest even, of the lower animals. For the perfection of animals, no such power of comprehension, as we have described, is needed. Their relations to the world are simple, and are fixed in the best manner by impulse. The relations of man, on the other hand, are of the most complex nature, so that it may be said, that each man has a mission, something to do in the world different from what every other one has to do.

New spheres of activity open before him, and as he enters each, there has often to be an entire new use of some lower activity, or an entire new adjustment of all the lower activities,—some being repressed which were formerly stimulated, and others brought into activity that were formerly kept in abeyance.

Now we can conceive of a being having all the lower activities, and the comprehension, that belongs to man, simply as a rational being, and these powers alone, with *will.* Such a being, with the capacity of enjoyment and suffering, through the sensibility connected with all these lower activities, would become, in his highest estate, a prudent being. Every act would be from his judgment of expediency in promoting pleasure or avoiding suffering. Everything would be reduced to the level of that action, by which a man cuts his wood in season to have it dry in winter, or puts his kindling in better shape and provides it in larger quantities, as the clouds and winds betoken increased cold. If he acted for children or friends, it would be from a natural impulse alone, as animals act in caring for their kind. With such beings the word *expedient* would be the highest in enforcing action; but, OUGHT, with the signification it now has, would be unknown.

Now, in man, we find another wonderful impulse to action making a part of his higher nature, and by which all the lower instincts and powers may be intensified in action, or be kept in abeyance. This is *Obligation*, or *the Sense of Obligation.* It is not only ultimate, like the impulses of the lower nature, but it is the highest impulse—ultimate in our analysis of man, as a moral being. As it belongs to man to comprehend the action of all his lower powers, and the use and proper limit of each one of them, this higher impulse grapples on to every one of them to restrain or quicken them. If, now, the knowledge of man were perfect, this Sense of Obligation would be a sure guide, and every act in accordance with its impulse would be the best possible. If the will were strong enough to secure every act that Obligation demands, man would be a perfect being. Mistake in action would be impossible. Perfect comprehension of the best relations, a sense of obligation to act in accordance with these relations, and strength of will to carry out the demands of Obligation, would be as perfect an outfit for man as we find in the animals, in their self-limiting and self-directing instincts. This outfit would be perfect in its action, but occupying a field where unlimited progress would not only be possible, but the natural result. It is the belief of many that man was created in this state. However that may be, he is in no such condition now. He makes sad mistakes, when he does the best he knows; and he weakly, or perversely, gives up to impulses which he knows ought to be restrained. If we were to judge by the results of human life alone, we should conclude that there is no law of man's being. For nothing can be greater than the differences of character between men of the same city and, oftentimes, of the same family. Searching for a law among so many discordant elements, to one compelled to judge of man's nature only from these results which he daily sees, would seem, at first, to be a hopeless task. Is man then without a law of his being which may guide him in his higher life? While animals have a law within them, which is like gravitation to the planets that guides them forever in their orbits, has man no impulse which will tend to direct his course? Are the best specimens of humanity, after all, only accidents? We think not. And we think that law and guide of action within man will be found in THE SENSE OF OBLIGATION, *when considered in all its demands,* and in relation to all the other provisions made for him.

LECTURE XI.

THE MORAL INSTINCTS—OBLIGATION.

Law of Being defined.—Relation of Men and animals to this law.—Conditions under which Obligation arises.—Man's Freedom.—Self-denial.—Effects of Ignorance.—Relation of Obligation to the Judgment.—Double action of Obligation.—Doing right because it is Right.—Obligation to do justly.—Four Manifestations of Obligation.—Its action compared with the Instincts.—Its relation to Progress.—Moral Conflicts.—Choice.—Free Personality.—Accountability.—Remorse.—Man compared with an animal.—Moral powers always found in him.—The perfection and sphere of the Animal.—The sphere of Man's Action.

WE have traced the instinctive principles, in man's animal nature, to find their method of action, and the means by which they are controlled. We have found these principles in him, capable of terrific power, and fitted by this power for efficient service, if they can be rightly directed. To find a controlling power for them, we are compelled to pass beyond the animal instincts themselves, to a higher nature. As the agency to enable man himself to guide and limit the action of his animal instincts, he needs a *Comprehending power*, to show him the relation of all his acts to results, and the relation of all subordinate results, to his highest good. He needs the *power of Choice*,—when different ends are comprehended,—in addition, to that executive volition, which he has, in common with the brutes,—and, last of all, he needs the *Sense of Obligation*, as the highest possible impulse to action.

It was suggested, in the last lecture, that we should find in the sense of obligation, considering all its *demands and relations*, the true law of human action, as we find in the lower instincts, the law of animal activity. And by the law of action, for any being, we mean *that within him, which guides, or tends to guide him, to that end for which he was made.* So men, as well as animals, have within them an impulse urging them to seek the end for which they were made, only men are left to learn what that end is, from the study of the impulse, and to guide themselves towards it, by the use of all their higher powers,—while the guidance to the animal comes from his organic development, and is towards an end, of which he knows nothing. We see, on every hand, the sufficiency of the instincts, as a guide to animals; while in man, these same instincts need control from some power beyond them. If we find Obligation to be such a controlling power, either alone or with the aid of other powers, we shall be satisfied.

It is not with us a question, now, how animals or man came by any of these powers. It is a question of possession, and of the nature and value of the possession.

Let us now try to find the facts in the case, without being bound by any preconceived notion or favorite definition.

In the first place, when two courses of action are

open before us, so that we can contemplate them and their results, there may arise a sense of obligation, for us to enter upon one course rather than the other.

This sense of obligation may be entirely distinct from any notion of expediency or pleasure to ourselves. It is undoubtedly true that the highest expediency and pleasure will ultimately be found in the line of obligation; but a conviction of this, is not necessary as a condition for the impulse of obligation. But it is also to be said that obligation always demands the good of the higher nature, when that is discerned, and the good of the higher nature never conflicts with the good of any other being.

The impulses of the animal nature impel us where present pleasure or animal enjoyment can be secured,—oftentimes against the good of others,—but obligation may demand that every *good* of our lower nature, even life itself, be sacrificed for the good of our higher. That is, the sense of obligation, so far as it acts from our contemplation of good, always demands that the animal in us be the servant of the human.

This sense of obligation is ever urging man on to discover the true end of his being and to attain it. But he has the power of going against this impulse, and of yielding himself to any one of the lower impulses of his nature, or we should not have true freedom; and he often goes against it, through ignorance or perverseness, in various ways, or we should have as uniform results in human life as among animals. Animal life reaches its end by a self-adjusting machinery so powerful as to control the animal. It is left to man alone to discover what the end of his being is, and then to act in conformity with the law that guides him towards that end, or against that law.

Man is under obligation to promote the greatest good of all beings, himself included. To yield obedience to this demand of obligation is one of the great acts of life, and one demanding what is called great self-denial; for it involves a constant struggle with all the lower propensities of our nature. Wise self-denial—all that is ever demanded and all that it is right for a man to make—is the control of any appetite or impulse when it conflicts with a higher good. This, even, may be like cutting off a right hand or plucking out a right eye.

But another great difficulty arises here, which follows every man through life,—the want of knowledge, which shall enable him to act in conformity to that high law of his being, which he knows to be good, and to which he may desire to conform.

The same thing is illustrated in the case of his body. He is compelled to suffer many things,—pain and sorrow and early death,—because, perchance, he ignorantly builds his house where poisons exhale from the earth. He may know that there is a law of health, but in attempting to follow it, his ignorance leads him into all sorts of pitfalls.

Has man then no guide towards the end of his being, before that end is comprehended as one securing the greatest good? We believe that the sense of obligation not only gives impulse to action, but that its *tendency* is to secure right action, even amidst the most disastrous mistakes of ignorance. This we think will appear before we close the discussion. And we now proceed to consider this sense of obligation still farther, in its subordinate operations to secure conformity to what would be its first great command, if man had wisdom enough to discover his true end from the beginning.

In the first place, the sense of obligation always arises to do a specific act, when that act is judged by us, to promote any end, the seeking of which obligation commands. It is no proof that the act will aid in securing the end, because the sense of obligation arises to perform it. If it were, man would need no aid from knowledge to guide his conduct in seeking any end that he knows to be good,—he would guide himself perfectly by the sense of obligation alone. All mistakes in seeking such an end would be impossible; and growth in knowledge would be useless as an aid in guiding moral action. There are those who make this fatal blunder in life. They satisfy "*conscience*," and through ignorance of relations commit hideous wrong, and call it God's service. Men may feel under obligation to do most wicked things, when they are ignorant, because the sense of obligation was never given to take the place of knowledge, or to be any excuse for ignorance.

The sense of obligation, as securing specific acts, has a certain fixed relation, then, to the *comprehending power*, or the judgments formed through the agency of that power. Let the judgment decide that a specific act will promote the great end, which it is the law of man's being to seek, and the sense of obligation to perform that act arises at once. The action of obligation is, in this sense, analogous to the action of the lower instinctive impulses. We have shown that they have a certain relation to the impression made upon the senses. Make a certain impression upon the senses of an animal, and the instinctive act follows, though its results may be the worst possible for the being. Animal Instinct was made to depend upon the senses for its light, or condition of acting, where it has any relation to the senses at all. In like manner, when the relation of a certain act, to the great end of our being, is judged to be direct, by the comprehending power of man, the sense of obligation to perform that act, arises at once, though the performance of it may, through ignorance of relations, involve the worst possible consequences. From this, it is plain that the impulse of obligation has the same relation to the comprehending power of man, that ordinary instinctive impulse has to simple sense-perception in animals.

Obligation then, we may regard as the great moral, instinctive impulse, that drives us to act in securing the greatest moral good at which man can aim, as the lower instinctive impulses drive animals and men to act to secure physical life, which to them, as mere animals, is the greatest good, as it is the condition of all good to them.

Both animal Instinct and the Sense of Obligation depend for their light, or condition of action, upon other powers. If it is instinct that preserves an animal, it is also true that it is through his instincts that we most easily destroy him. Deceive his senses, and he will destroy himself, by his own instinctive act. That which was made to preserve him, becomes the surest means of his destruction.

So the worst acts the world has ever witnessed, have been performed under the stimulus of Obligation, arising from mistaken views of relations. The persecutions, the burnings and stonings,—the martyrdoms in all ages,—are the horrid work of this highest instinct, guided by ignorance. It is like the power that drives the engine safely on its way, when the road is in perfect order, but which brings ruin and death, when the rails are broken or misplaced.

Obligation demands results in accordance with the great end of man's being, which it constantly enforces, and ever keeps potentially present as the basis of every act; as the love of life is present as the basis of every lower instinctive act. But it has, of itself, no power to comprehend the relations which will secure the best results. For this light, or condition of right action, it must depend upon the comprehending power, whether that be INTELLECT, REASON or MORAL REASON, or all of these combined,

But this action of Obligation alone would plainly be defective as an aid in reaching the great end which it commands us to seek. It can go with safety, only as the comprehending power furnishes the conditions, and this furnishes the conditions by investigating all agencies, and the tendencies of all courses of action; that is, the great work of the comprehending power, is to gather knowledge from every source open to it, to enable it to furnish the right conditions, so that every act, which Obligation demands shall be towards the great end which it constantly impels us to seek. If knowledge were perfect, so that the exact relation of every act to the great end of life, were fully understood, the machinery would be perfect, as we have said. But there is great ignorance of the relation of acts to results, and of results to the chief end of life. If the whole work of obligation, as a means to this end, were simply to impel to acts in view of perceived relations, it is evident that a man might remain in ignorance, and still obey the voice of Obligation, while constantly working against the supreme end which she commands him to seek. Obligation might be constantly commanding him to do specific acts, contrary to her original and generic command, as though a father who had commanded his son to raise wheat, should then command him to sow the seed on ground unfit for that kind of grain, or to sow in midsummer, or to parch the seed before sowing.

Plainly, if man were left with a constitution like this, the worst consequences would follow practically, and Reason would never justify the Creator in giving such a constitution to any being.

But now we find Obligation doing another work, which has a tendency to correct this defect, so that its work can be justified by Reason. While it acts, in view of relations discovered by the comprehending power, and of results which that power declares to be in the direction of the great end first commanded, it also demands of the comprehending power that it do its work in the most faithful manner. While Obligation must have light from the comprehending power, it does not wait for that light to come or not, as some lower impulse may determine, but with royal voice, it demands more light every instant of time,—it demands all the light the comprehending power can give,—it will be satisfied with nothing less, and it increases its demands, as the capacity of the comprehending power increases, when used in the best manner possible. Can any thing be more beautiful than this *double action* of obligation in the system of means? It does not make man a perfect being, as to knowledge, but it is beautiful, as the means of constant progress towards perfection. There is resting upon man, evermore, the obligation to do right, and to secure knowledge, that he may know what right is.

But are we done with Obligation yet? We think not. In its action just referred to, we have taken it for granted that the action was based upon the decision of the comprehending power,—whether correct or not,—that the result aimed at was in the direction of the great end of life, *the end for which man was made*. But it must be plain to every one, that we are not compelled either to make broad generalizations, to understand the great end of life, or the relation of every act to the greatest good of all men, or the glory of God, before we have the impulse of Obligation to act, this fact has been clearly seen by moral philosophers, and it has been fully considered by them. Obligation is found enforcing certain subordinate acts, as those of justice, mercy and truth, even when the good secured by them is not taken into account; and we even find it enforcing certain acts, as those of justice or honesty, when the act cannot be justified to Reason, at the time, as producing or tending to produce, the greatest good. And, undoubtedly, on this account, has arisen much controversy about "*doing right because it is right*." It means, we suppose, that the sense of Obligation impels us to perform certain acts, that may seem at the time opposed to the greatest good, if we mean by that the greatest happiness of all. That it does this, we suppose all will admit. A single illustration will show the principle. If I have property in my hands belonging to a rich man, who can never need it—who already has more than is needed by him, so that my judgment and the judgment of others, himself included, is that he would be happier if he had less, and I am in want so that the property would add to my happiness, there is yet a sense of justice, which prevents my appropriating the property. I feel under obligation to restore that property to him, though I need it for my comfort, and he does not need it for his. That sense of obligation to return him his own, does not yield to any prospect of advantage to me in retaining it, until a new principle comes in—the saving of life. I feel under obligation to save that, at the expense of all property that I can use, whether my own or another's.

Now that sense of justice, and the accompanying sense of obligation to do justly, are so essential to the welfare of such a being as man is, and so essential as a part of the means for carrying out that social and moral system which the highest Reason justifies, that they seem to be both given to man to secure the action which is right in reference to his highest end, even when there is no conception of the good which they were intended to produce,—as the instincts were given to the lower animals, to secure certain actions essential to the life of the individual or species, though the animal could have no conception of the relation of the act to the ultimate end to be attained.

It is this kind of impulse, from a sense of obligation to perform certain acts, the good of which we do not see, and which the judgment, at the time, even pronounces against as a means of producing the greatest happiness, that probably gives rise to the notion that we feel under obligation to "do right because it is right." *It is plain that we feel under obligation to do certain acts, for the doing of which we can give no reason except that we feel the obligation.* And we shall find all such acts to be of so fundamental a character, that it would be ruinous to any system of moral government, if not destructive to the race, to leave them to arouse the sense of obligation only when the production of good is asserted of them by the judgment. But the acts that follow this sense of obligation thus originating, are, in their relation to a moral system, and the highest end of man as connected with that system, like those instinctive acts in the lower animals, without which the species could not exist, and the necessity of which it would be impossible for them to learn from experience. It is difficult to see how acts thus performed, are higher in their nature than those that are preceded by Obligation founded on comprehension of relations and rational choice.

We thus have these four possible manifestations of obligation.

FIRST,—As requiring man to choose the end for which he was made, when that is comprehended.

SECOND,—As impelling him to every act that is judged to be a means of securing that end.

THIRD,—Impelling to certain acts when no relation is, at the time, perceived between them and that ultimate end which, when comprehended, obligation commands us to seek.

FOURTH,—As laying its constant and ever increasing demands upon the comprehending power to furnish the best conditions for its action.

In all these respects its analogy to animal Instinct is very striking and beautiful,—Obligation having for its aim the spiritual, or higher life of man, as the instincts of animals relate to the physical life.

FIRST,—The leading instinctive impulses of animals, are those which demand the preservation of life—the life of the individual and the continuance of the species.

SECOND,—There is an instinctive impulse to do all things that are seen to be connected with the preservation of the individual or the species.

THIRD,—There is an impulse to do certain acts which, as the animal performs them, have no perceived relation to the end to be secured by them.

FOURTH,—These instinctive impulses make constant demands upon the senses to furnish the light, or condition which they need for their best action.

It may aid us in making the comparisons, to bring the different points together.

1. OBLIGATION is given to secure the perfection of the higher life of the individual and the race, which is the highest good to both.

INSTINCT of animals, is to secure the preservation of physical life, which is the greatest good to them, and the condition of all good.

2. OBLIGATION impels to every act that secures, or is judged to secure, the highest good of the individual or race.

INSTINCT impels to every act that tends to secure the life of the individual, or species.

3. OBLIGATION impels to certain acts, though they may not be seen by us at the time, to lead to the greatest good.

INSTINCT impels to certain acts not seen by the animal, at the time, to have any relation to the continuance of life.

4. OBLIGATION depends upon the comprehending power for its light, or condition for right action.

INSTINCT depends upon the senses for the conditions of its action.

This is another of those marked instances where the method of action continues the same in different planes of activity, even when the powers acting in one plane are entirely distinct, in kind, from those acting in the other.

Obligation and animal Instinct differ, especially in this, that obligation depending for its conditions on the comprehending power, is fitted for an unlimited range of progress; or the being possessing it has progressive capacity constantly increasing in the individual and gaining new light from generation to generation, and from the observation and experience of thousands, at the same time,—while animal Instinct, having its condition from the bodily senses, has but limited range in the individual, and the individual can gain nothing from those that have gone before him, and but little from those associated with him. There is connected with animal Instinct, no such system of progress as is connected with Obligation, if there is any at all. We have, thus far, spoken of the impulse of Obligation, as though men follow it as certainly as animals follow the impulses of their Instinct. But this is far from being the case. If they did, there would be a uniformity of moral action, and of results in the higher life of man, that would approach the uniformity of animal life secured by Instinct. The moral acts of men would differ only as their knowledge differed. They might make mistakes, but intentional wrong-doing would be impossible.

Man has a truly animal nature with all the impulses of animal appetites and instincts. He has, also, this higher nature, in which the sense of Obligation is the great impulse. As this higher nature in man is the natural ruler of the other in him, there is often conflict between them. The lower impulses draw in one direction, while Obligation forbids the advance, or even demands an entirely different line of action. If this were not so, man would know nothing of those moral conflicts which he now finds going on within him. An animal may, by its nature, be impelled or compelled, to fight another; but as a moral being, a man's severest battles are with himself,—between his higher and lower nature.

When the lower impulses are in one direction, and the impulse of Obligation in another, the condition of CHOICE is presented. And rational choice is involved, in every act which follows the Sense of Obligation, *when that arises from a comprehension of results.* As the first demand of Obligation is that the highest end of man should be chosen, when that end is comprehended, so the first rational, generic choice is the choice of that end, as the goal towards which every power must press. That act of choice declares that the lower nature shall, henceforth, be the servant of the higher,—it shall be well used, that it may be a good servant, but the doom of its servitude is pronounced, once for all. The man henceforth rules himself,—all the animal nature within him is in subjection. Such a choice is the act of FREE PERSONALITY. It cannot be illustrated, because there is nothing else like it. It is the only point of true freedom. It is known by consciousness alone. Every act of choice, both generic and specific, may be in the line that Obligation requires, or it may be opposed to it. Every choice involving Obligation, or subsequent to the impulse of Obligation, whether in accordance with it or against it, is a decision between the higher and lower nature, and determines which of them shall, for the time, rule. *It is in the power of this intelligent choice, that we discover the highest freedom, the only true freedom, and it is here that we see the ground of man's accountability.*

The impulse of Obligation being given to secure the right, or most effective, use of all our powers, it may extend to every act towards ourselves, our fellow-men and God. As it is ultimate, in the sense of having no impulse to action higher than itself, it has connected with it a fearful power, by which it enforces its commands. It has nothing above it to restrain its action; and it never needs restraint, but only light, that it may act in the right direction. Then the best results come from the full measure of its activity. In this respect, it is, in its action, analogous to the instincts of animals, which unconstrained work out the best results for them, provided the senses furnish the proper condition of action.

As there is nothing above Obligation to restrain it, so there is nothing to aid it as an impulse. It secures its own effective action only by its own constitution, if at all. Remorse is the recoil of this great impulse to action, in the higher nature of man, when its action is thwarted by the power of the lower instincts, which were not made to rule.

If any act is contrary to the demands of Obligation, the punishment that follows is quick and intense. If the act is as Obligation demands, there is, at the time, no recoil, although the act, through ignorance, may produce the worst results. There may be sorrow for the unfortunate results, but no remorse. But if the judgment, afterwards, decides that the ignorance which caused the evil was unnecessary, then remorse follows, as though the Sense of Obligation had been violated at the time of performing the act. For it is a part of the office of Obligation, as we have shown, to secure from the comprehending power all the light it can give.

There must be an apprehension of one's relation to an act, before Obligation can arise. Then there must be consciousness of the Obligation. CONSCIENCE then, or *moral consciousness*, grasps by an intuitive comprehension every relation of man to every act involving choice between the impulses of the higher and lower nature; and in connection with every such act contrary to the sense of Obligation, there comes the punishment of remorse, which we conceive to be the dreadful recoil of this highest moral impulse, Obligation, when it is defied and thwarted in its legitimate work. It is Conscience or moral consciousness, that makes the torments of remorse possible; and if one chooses to regard obligation and remorse both as the work of Conscience, we do not object, as we are seeking for facts, and not for theoretical divisions or definitions.

We are now prepared to state the difference between a man and an animal, as we have found them in our analysis, up to this point. It consists in three things.

In man we find—

FIRST,—A comprehending power, that surveys the universe, and all the capacities of its possessor, in relation to that universe.

SECOND,—A sense of Obligation to do certain acts, and to refrain from others,—this sense arising spontaneously, in view of certain relations or results, and being distinct from those impulses of the affections or desires, which may belong to an animal.

THIRD,—The power of choice, that gives, by its generic action, individuality of aim for a lifetime; and, in specific acts, determines whether the higher or lower nature of man shall rule. These three powers, with executive volition, make man the ruler of the world and the shaper of his own destiny, so far as choice and attempts are concerned.

These three powers are all that we have yet found distinctive in the higher nature of man. If animals have either of them, we look in vain for the proof of it in the whole range of the animal kingdom. It is claimed by some that animals have these powers, but the proof offered is not satisfactory. The beautiful action of the natural instincts, as the social instincts, and parental instincts,—is often triumphantly referred to as proof of the moral nature of animals; but a full analysis of these instincts shows that they occupy an entirely different sphere from the three powers we have mentioned. In man these natural instincts call the moral nature into action, it is true; but in the animals, they need neither guidance nor restraint from obligation or any thing above them, as we have shown.

But an animal may have, and probably does have, other emotions which are so intimately related to the moral nature, as instruments, as to be readily mistaken for its essential powers, or characteristics. An animal may have the emotion of pity, and also an impulse that secures justice, so far as it is essential to animal life. They, certainly, instinctively act as though they had such emotions. It may be that they have only a simple impulse, that secures the proper action, while in man, there may precede every one of his acts, comprehension, the sense of of Obligation, and choice. If we say that Obligation can only follow comprehension of ends, then we must allow that the simple impulses, which secure justice, truth and the like, are in the same line as Obligation would require, were there comprehension of the results, and so like it in every respect as to be distinguished from it with great difficulty.

If animals have a comprehension of moral relations, with the accompanying sense of Obligation, and that consciousness of the comprehension of relations and sense of obligation, which is *Conscience* itself, or the product of *Conscience*, we see no proof of it. We can account for all their actions, perfectly, by referring to some lower principle of instinctive impulse, which in them is self-directive.

All men give evidence that they have all these elements, which can be reckoned as belonging to conscience. They may be in a wretched state of activity, through ignorance; or the scale of humanity may be so low that animal impulses seem to have the entire sway, and thus moral distinctions may have made no impression on the language of degraded tribes. But this no more proves that these moral powers are not present, than the absence of algebraic language and methods, among ignorant men, is proof that such men have no power to generalize in numbers. Whenever search has been made for the elements of conscience in man, they have been found. They are at least potentially present, as the blade is present in the grain of corn. The work of missionaries in all parts of the world abundantly proves this.

We see, then, that the moral nature of man is all that it could be, and leave him a free and progressive being.

All the wretchedness of the world comes from two things, *from ignorance of the relations of acts to the great end of life, and that strange perverseness which leads men to choose against the sense of Obligation.* If both of these evils were remedied, man would still be a free, progressive being, as new relations and conditions of activity opened before him; but his choices always being according to Obligation, and his comprehension of all new relations being perfect, his course would be like that of a ship, when it moves in a direct line from port to port; while now he is at best, like a ship that makes its way midst fogs, and darkness, and adverse winds. And, too often, the pilot deserts the helm, leaving the ship to float, as the winds and currents chance to move. This condition of the race, all see and acknowledge. As to the final result of this condition, and as to the remedy for it, there is great disagreement. It does not come within our province to seek for a remedy, or to declare that none is needed. It was our business in making this survey of the instinctive principles, to find their position in man, as a being able to guide himself, through his higher nature,—to contrast his condition with that of animals, which are guided by those appetites and instincts which man is called upon to guide and limit in himself.

Here, then, we close our discussion in relation to man, as belonging to this world alone. He has a physical system, with senses and reflexive movements, as the animals have. He has appetites and instincts like theirs in kind, but differing from theirs in degree, as theirs differ among the various species. He has instincts also,—such as we see no trace of in them,—which relate to the progress of society. He has a comprehending power capable of understanding his relations to the universe, and the power of choice in selecting his line of action, in the world. He has, with this power, the Sense of Obligation, which impels him to act, and punishes him if he does not; and at the same time it impels him to obtain the knowledge necessary for reaching the results that secure the highest good. He suffers from ignorance; and this shows that he is not a perfect being now, even in the agencies which secure progress. His nobleness is seen in the outfit given him, which forbids him to remain in ignorance, and enables him to improve by the experience and labors of all the generations before him.

The perfection of the animal will appear in every one of the species, if his activities have full play. That there shall be such uniformity of excellence, among members of the human race, if not impossible, is something for many generations yet to come to aim at. There have, thus far, in every age, been those whose higher nature ruled. They might be wanting in some kinds of knowledge, but they had reached the highest plane of action which it is possible for man to reach. There have been others, who have given themselves up to their bodily appetites and instincts. This is the lowest plane of action to which man can sink. He is then vastly lower, in his actions, than the brutes can be, because his animal propensities have no such limitation and self-guidance, as theirs have.

The works of an animal are for himself and those associated with him, or to spring from him. The works of man are for generations to come, and often for those of foreign and even hostile nations. The animal acts best when he acts as his appetites and instincts impel. Man feels all these impulses, and has, in addition, the Sense of Obligation, as an impulse, that may work with them or against them; and which he must obey, in all its commands, or suffer its immediate and terrible punishment.

When we have considered the religious instincts of man, we can mark other differences between him and the highest of the lower animals, as we shall then have other elements of character that belong only to him.

LECTURE XII.

RELIGIOUS INSTINCTS. — SUMMARY AND CONCLUSION.

Summary of principles.— Their existence denied.—May be dormant.—Assert their sway.—Knowledge of God.—Instinct of a child.—Natural Religion.—Revelation.—Instinct of Prayer.—Of Worship.—Analogous to Animal Instincts.—Individual Accountability.—Diagram of Powers.—Explanation of Activities.—Choice of an Ultimate End.—Provisions for every Appetite and Desire.—Summary of Lectures.—Defects of our Education.—Man's power over the Universe.—His relationship to it.—Prepare the way for Progress.— The Laborers needed.—Influence of names.— Transition Period.—Final results of the study and control of all the Powers.

WE have considered man in his animal nature, as possessing appetites and instincts which act without a guiding power in them or among them. We have also shown the relation of this animal nature to a higher nature, which is fitted to control it, and has, as its own possession, the means—by automatic powers and free-personality—of controlling itself. All of these powers thus balanced, would justify themselves to Reason, if this world and the physical life of man were their only sphere of action, and the limit of their duration in each individual. But there is a whole group of emotions, aspirations and impulses, which seem to be meaningless, if man's conscious activity is limited to the duration of his physical life, and there is no Intelligent Being above him who has personal relations to him.

It is in order now for us to enumerate these active principles, of what may be called the *Religious nature* of man, in distinction from his *Moral*, and to point out their analogy to the lower instinctive principles. It is the work of the Natural Theologian, to interpret these principles fully and to pronounce upon their value or worthlessness to man.

These instinctive principles are—

1. Belief in some supernatural being—or beings.

2. Belief in accountability, or relationship to that being in such measure as for good or evil to come from it.

3. Belief in immortality, and the continuance of this relation after death.

4. The Instinct of prayer, as a means of establishing relations with this being.

5. The Instinct of worship, including the emotion of veneration and its expression.

The existence of these beliefs and impulses as something essential to humanity, has been denied, and they are in some cases so dormant or weak through the degradation of the man, that like some of the lower instinctive principles, they do not make themselves known to observers till the proper conditions are applied for bringing them into special activity. In proof of their universality, we can only appeal to the present condition of the race.*

These principles assert their sway over those who, as speculative philosophers, have denied their

* See Appendix—Note A.

existence, and they appear in some form in every religion from the highest to the lowest. And when men wonder at the number of religions and the absurd notions connected with religious practices, they would do well to remember that all these are manifestations of the instincts or impulses of a religious nature. They prove that man has such impulses. And that is all we wish now to show. We are not called upon to show that these impulses are either useless or of the highest importance, though we are permitted to state our belief that they are the highest instinctive impulses of our nature,—that Obligation enters this field to strengthen every impulse to action—and that one of the most reasonable of all things, from the analogy of nature, is to expect that the means of satisfying these instincts will be provided for man.

This instinctive belief in the existence of a God, has never of itself proved to be directive, so as to give a knowledge of God directly, that Reason could approve of. The knowledge of God, so far as man has gained it for himself, has come from the comprehending power,—either from that portion of it called Pure Reason, evolving necessary notions of an absolute, perfect being ; or it has come as a necessary induction from the contemplation of the works of nature, including the constitution of man. From this intellectual notion of God, there would be gradually gained by the study of God's works, a knowledge of his character ; and from that character, inferences could be rationally drawn as to his relations to man and what he would do for him.

The probability of a Revelation in words, would be settled, and the proper tests of such a Revelation would be determined. So that, in the end, man's Reason would be satisfied as to the existence of God, His character, and relations to man, and the nature and extent of His Communications to him. All such knowledge would be of slow growth, and it is evident that if religion depended solely upon such knowledge, it could only be in the later and more perfect forms of society that an adequate knowledge of God could be reached, or that a Revelation could be so tested by Reason as to be accepted on rational grounds.

But in distinction from all this, there is in man the Instinct of a child, or of a dependent towards some Unseen Power. This instinct manifests itself as a power in all races of men, so that religion does not begin as a product of Reason, or as a result of induction from the study of the works of nature. This impulse, or this instinctive belief, has been so strong as to give rise to the numberless gods of the heathen, and to belief in oracles, auguries, signs and visions, for the guidance of man. They have all been believed in, because they are such manifestations in kind as this instinct leads man to expect. They have been accepted in all their crudities, because the comprehending Power of man has not done its appropriate work in giving the light and guidance to this instinct, which it ought to furnish. It plainly has but two methods of giving light on this subject. The first is through the study of nature, — or *Natural Religion;* and the second through *Revelation,* which it can test, as to its source, and consequent validity. It would lead us too far from our subject to follow the baffled strivings of this instinct, in seeking by itself alone the satisfaction of its own yearnings. But there are certain beliefs joined with this instinct that are like special instinctive impulses. The first is the belief in accountability to this unseen Being; and the second is belief in immortality, which carries the accountability beyond this life.

The third manifestation of instinct correlated with the belief in God, and accountability,—or of His personal relation to us,—is *Prayer.* The instinct of prayer is the most manifest of all the religious instincts, and is more nearly self-directive than any other of them; and it is so strong, that, at times, it breaks through every philosophical theory of necessity, or pantheism, or atheism itself.

But in the addition to the impulse of prayer, is that of adoration,—of *worship.* There is in this no servile fear; but there may be awe. There may be no desire of favor, but a pouring out of the soul, in adoration and praise, which has no end beyond what is found in the act itself, as meeting a demand of our nature. It is the gratification of an instinct, which forms a part of the original constitution of man.

In all these things,—belief in God, in immortality, in accountability, and in having the instinctive impulses of prayer and praise *towards an unseen Being,*—man stands alone, so far as we can judge.

These instinctive beliefs and the instinctive actions are strongly analogous to some found in the lower animals, and almost a perfect type of the instincts of a child towards a parent. But having reference to an *unseen Being* and reaching towards another life, they are peculiar. They are, however, in this, analogous to the instincts of such animals as provide for the future, of which they can know nothing by inference, either from their own past experience, or from any knowledge gained from those of their kind. The analogy holds in regard to action respecting an unknown future, but these principles and the instincts, in other respects, are entirely unlike. The latter relate to the continuance of the species, or the comfort of the individual, while the former relate to accountability,—*individual accountability to God*,—which Webster said was the greatest thought he ever had. We have reached, then, in the instincts of the religious nature, the origin of the highest thoughts, and the most powerful impulses to action through love or fear. And as understanding gives direction to these impulses, by itself or through revelation, we find the authority of obligation joined with them to secure them from defeat by the lower nature.

We are now prepared to give a diagram that shall aid in showing the comparative condition of all the powers possessed in common by men and animals—it being understood that the word "INSTINCT" only marks the *beginning* of that kind of activity which is continued in some form among all the higher powers.

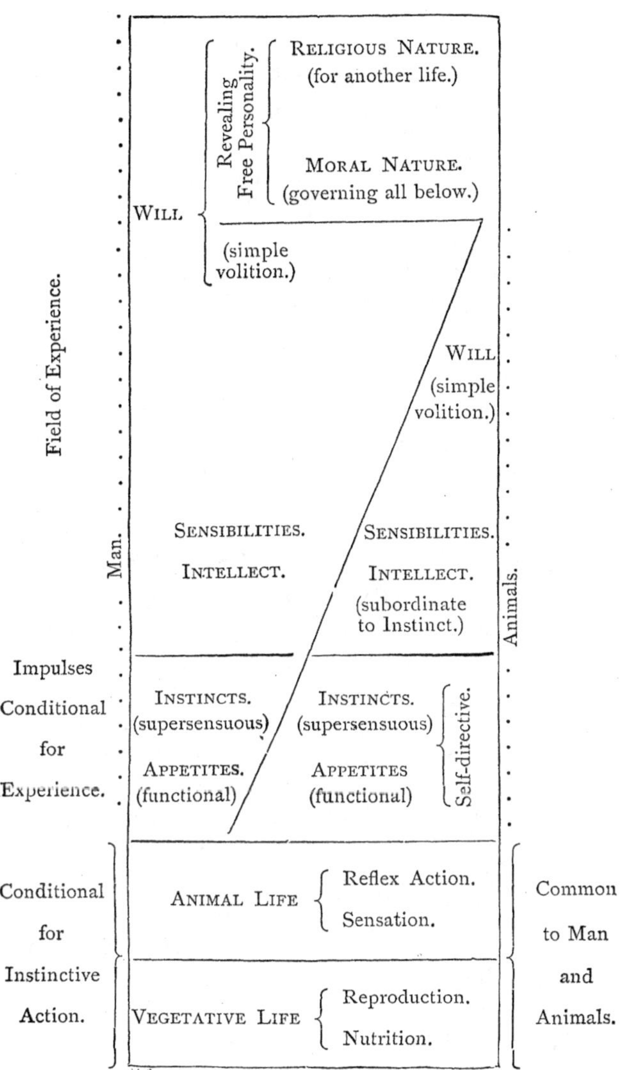
Field of Experience.
Man.
WILL
Revealing Free Personality.
RELIGIOUS NATURE.
(for another life.)
MORAL NATURE.
(governing all below.)
(simple volition.)
WILL
(simple volition.)
SENSIBILITIES.
INTELLECT.
SENSIBILITIES.
INTELLECT.
(subordinate to Instinct.)
Animals.
Impulses Conditional for Experience.
INSTINCTS.
(supersensuous)
APPETITES.
(functional)
INSTINCTS.
(supersensuous)
APPETITES
(functional)
Self-directive.
Conditional for Instinctive Action.
ANIMAL LIFE
Reflex Action.
Sensation.
VEGETATIVE LIFE
Reproduction.
Nutrition.
Common to Man and Animals.

It is impossible for any diagram to adequately represent the complex powers of man or of animals in all their relations,—for the lowest powers are often united in action with the highest,—but it may do something to aid us in gaining a connected view of the activities which we have investigated, so far as our purpose required that we should investigate them.

We find at the basis of all activity, in animals and men, the *vegetative life*, by which the body is sustained and the species continued. Next to this, comes the truly *animal nature*, as the condition for sensation, reflex action, and sense-perceptions. All these must be common to men and animals, as the condition for instinctive action. In addition to this machinery, we want impulse to action. And as the first impulse to instinctive action, or one of the first, we have the appetites which arise from the functional activity of organs. They belong to the vegetative life, but involve sensations and have no direct dependence upon the will. Next in order we have certain Instincts, which *minister* to these appetites, or in other words, the animal has, as an original gift, the knowledge and skill needed to enable him to properly satisfy his appetites; and this original knowledge and skill constitute animal Instinct,—Instinct in its lowest plane of action.

We have regarded Instinct when used as a *general term*, as simply a name for the peculiar action of various powers; and have shown that so far as any animal is wanting in any instinct or power, in the beginning of life, to care for himself, the lack is supplied by the Instinct of the parent.

But since the Appetites are not sufficiently broad to furnish impulses for all the action needed for animals of high rank, we have the *Desires*, so called, which do not rise from any function of the body. These give rise to whole series of instinctive activities, of special kinds. And so here we find instinctive action rising into a higher plane than the mere satisfying of Appetite.

The Appetites and *Instinctive impulses*, and the Instincts which guide action specifically, are the necessary provision made for every being that is to have an experience. Sometimes the instincts take the place of experience entirely,—they always must involve so much of original knowledge and skill as are needful for carrying on the work of life, until experience can be gained to aid in the work.

Above these instincts is *Intellect*, by which the being comprehends relations and the results of its own acts. In the animal, this is so low, or rather so weak, as to be subordinated to the instincts of the body. In man it is the servant of a higher nature, which by the aid of the intellect subordinates and controls the instincts of the body.

In both animals and men are found *Sensibility and will.*—Sensibility in man, taking a very wide range, compared with that in animals,—its highest range being beyond his animal nature, into the moral and religious. *Will* in the animal seems to be merely the obedient executive, carrying out the suggestions of the instinctive powers; while in man, it performs the same office work, and is also the power, by which every appetite, instinct and desire, may be held in check at the bidding of his higher nature. In connection with this office of Will, in man, the *power of choice* is manifested,—CHOICE OF AN ULTIMATE END FOR LIFE, or the line of activity for life, which determines each man's position in the world, so far as it is possible for him to break through the bounds, which physical organization prescribes for him. It gives individuality among men, from some principle superior to physical organization, and hence the diversity of human life. We honor or despise men for what they are through their own choice.

We can discover no power like this in the animal. His position is marked out for him by his structure and instincts. He has no power to learn the history of the past, or to contemplate the possibilities of the distant future, and then train himself, by years of labor and self-denial, for the conflict. This power man has.

Passing still higher, we find the *Moral Nature*, with its great central impulse, OBLIGATION, which governs, or ought to govern, all the powers below it. It is to the higher nature of man what the bodily instincts are in animals, except that in man, Intellect must give the knowledge needful to direct, and Will the limitation of action. So that every act of man from the impulse of Obligation involves the exercise of free personality.

Knowledge of *relations through the Power of Comprehension*, the *Sense of Obligation arising in view of that comprehension, and the Power of Choice, in accordance with Obligation, or against it, are the attributes of a* PERSON. Nothing like this combination of powers is found in the animal, nor is it needed. The natural impulses and instincts of the animal, are limited by the functions of the body, to certain periods, or to a given degree of strength, so that they are self-regulative and need no limiting power above them. In man, they are mainly impulses indicating direction, but their limitation must come from the man himself. They bring ruin to him before they limit themselves.

Still higher, we find the *Religious Nature*, that joins this life to another. It gives hopes of immortality, belief in a Father's care, and sends the desires of the heart up in prayer to Him. If there is not another life, if there is not a Power that can answer to our cry, then the Religious nature of man is such a blunder as we find in no other part of creation. Every appetite, desire, and instinct, below, has something responsive to it. They are all given, because there is something in the universe that answers to them. The insect deposits her egg in autumn, because the earth is to move on hundreds of millions of miles, and bring the spring time with warmth and leaves for her young. So every animal instinct is answered.

Shall we believe that this Religious nature is a mockery? and that, in answer to all these instincts, there is no Father to listen when we call? no love to succor, and no light and blessedness beyond the grave? The heavens and the earth in their adaptation to the nature of every plant and animal on the globe, cry out against such a belief. As we find provisions in our earth rising in *kind* for every animal and man, as their wants rise to higher planes, we accept these provisions as proof that He, who has cared for myriads of beings below us, and for us to this point, has not mocked us in regard to this one great provision which our highest nature demands.

We have thus discussed, so far as we have been able, the topics presented in our first lecture, as the programme of our work, which we now bring to a close.

We considered first, the operations in inorganic nature, foreshadowing Instinct.

Here we found, in the structure of the earth, the constitution of air and water, the change of seasons, and chemical changes of the soil, the same kind of provision for all organic beings, as are made by instinctive knowledge and skill in the animal kingdom.

Entering then the organic kingdom, the simulation of instinct was more clearly shown in the operations of all plant life and in the physiological changes of the animal body.

We next came to the simple instincts, that care for the body, supplementing structure and function of organs, so that the work begun within the body may be carried on in a wider sphere than structure and function alone can reach. These simple forms of Instinct were found to have the Appetites as their impulses.

But these were not broad enough for all the demands of animal life; and to meet these demands of wider range, we found impulses, or desires and instincts, arising beyond the sphere of any specific organization. Among the instinctive acts arising from such impulses, we found the migration of animals, the storing of food for winter and the fear of special enemies.

We next traced the instincts related to special structures, and those necessary for the existence of certain communities of animals. So much we found needful for adult individuals. But nature cares also for the species; in fact, among the lower animals the care of the individual seems to have constant reference to the preservation of the species.

Here we found three distinct topics for discussion,—the instincts of the young, to bring them into relation with their parents and the world,—instincts, which, like those of the gall-fly, demand certain changes in other objects to complete their work,—and the peculiar instincts of one stage of being, preparatory to another, as seen in the development of insects from the lowest form to the highest. We then treated of the variation of instinct, through the abnormal conditions of domestication, and of instinct, as the Law of animal life.

At this point we gave a summary, showing Instinct not to be the manifestation of any peculiar principle, but to be simply a method of action common to all beings and to all their powers, in a certain stage of their activity, — involving that impulse, knowledge and skill, which the being must have as an original gift, as a basis for experience; as it must have a certain organization of the body, as a basis for independent growth. We also showed that Nature gives as little Instinct to all beings as possible, and leaves the rest to experience. But if experience is impossible, then she completes the work by Instinct.

We then treated of Intelligence among animals,—of Intelligence as the servant of Instinct, thus accounting for the uniform plane of life in each species of the animal kingdom.

Next we considered the animal Instincts proper of man, and then his higher Instincts or Desires, finding in them the basis of his social nature.

And last of all, we have treated of the Moral and Religious Instincts, and have found in Obligation the great controlling instinctive impulse which modifies all others in man.

This work we have done, as we announced that we should do it, mainly in the service of man. We have not forgotten that the lower animals are sentient beings,—that many of them have a high capacity for enjoyment and suffering. When we remember that the lower tribes alone inhabited this earth for long ages,—compared with which, the highest antiquity claimed for man is but as yesterday,—we cannot regard mere animal enjoyment of the brute creation as insignificant, in the plan of creation. And whatever enters into that plan, is worthy of the thought and study of man. But the capacity for bodily suffering cannot be greater in the animal than in man; and the bodily suffering of man, is as nothing, compared with his capacity to suffer in

With all our boasted reforms and advance in government, education and religion, the degradation and suffering that fill the dark places of the earth are the inheritance of man, and not of the lower animals. And this degradation comes from ignoring or transgressing the law of man's being,—by giving loose rein to the animal appetites and Instincts, or by attempting to repress them without reason. We must come to a more thorough study of man. This study must take no secondary place in our systems of education, not even in the "NEW EDUCATION." We have been forgetting that the highest knowledge for man is a knowledge of his own powers, and of his relations to the whole universe and to God; we have taught, at least by practice, that the highest knowledge is found in the study of Natural Science, in its practical applications, and in the laws of trade. We have often dignified mere aggregated facts, of local value, with the name of science, and have thought more of controlling steam-engines than of controlling the powers of men or of teaching men the necessity of controlling themselves, and the methods of doing the work. We have sent them out to study the world, but have failed to show them how they are linked to it, and how they ought to rise above its power by, first of all, obeying its demands. It is only through a knowledge of physical laws and of his own nature, in all its planes, especially in that plane of instinctive impulses where activities arise and strive without his bidding, and in spite of his Will, —it is only through this broad knowledge of self, strive without his bidding, and in spite of his Will, —it is only through this broad knowledge of self, that man can bring every power into service, and make it minister to the great work of life which he has made the object of his choice. He is linked by an iron fate to this universe, but so linked that, through the aid of his higher powers, he may make the whole material universe his servant, almost as readily as he can control his own body. Can he not whisper around the globe, as easily as across the room? Do not the stars and compass tell him his pathway on the ocean? Does he not, while he sleeps, travel with a steed that cannot tire? Can he not pluck the fruits of far off lands as readily as those that grow in his own garden? Can he not see the storm a thousand miles away and prepare for its coming?

It is because all nature has, or may have, relations to man,—because he is acted upon by every force, and related to all the changes of the organic and inorganic world,—that the study of nature is of any value. The whole physical universe is seen to centre in him. What problem of the past geologic ages can be studied, that does not, in some way, bear upon the question of man's origin or destiny? The Botanist and Zoölogist may study abortive stamens, or forms of birds' nests, but they cannot, in this day, disconnect even these from some theory of man. The astronomer may watch the stars, measure the craters of the moon, analyze the blazing tongues of fire that encircle the sun, but no conclusion he reaches is complete till its relation to the past, present or future of man, is determined.

Man is the one point towards which all the rays of light in the physical universe seem to converge. And whatever ray is struck by the searcher for truth, if he follows its direction, man is his ultimate goal. We may believe that this relationship has been established by the direct and repeated interference of Creative Power and Intelligence; or we may believe, if we can, that it has come from some law of the universe, which from nebulous matter, has evolved all past and present forms of life; but the fact of man's universal relationship still remains.

We announced, in the beginning of this course, that it was no part of our plan to discuss theories of development, which attempt to account for the origin of the relations among organic beings. We have referred to them, only incidentally. Our work has been, mainly, to find how things are, what the relations are, which the instinctive principles of action now establish between the animal kingdom and the world around it, and especially, the position of these principles in man. We have found it impossible to study these, without showing their relation to every class of powers which man possesses. *And so complex is man,—so linked together are all his activities,—they so act together in every effort he puts forth,—that he must be studied as a whole, before any one portion of his nature can be fully understood.* Each portion of his nature has relations to the others, and he has relations to the world, upon which his whole activity depends.

It has unfortunately happened that too many have attempted to study man, without due attention to these relationships. Some have placed man in a world of their own creation, that does not correspond to the world of reality. Others have studied him from a single stand point, in physical science. Others, still, have ignored the truly animal nature, which is the agency through which man works, and by which he may be controlled.

The result of all such partial study of his nature, has been unfortunate,—unfortunate for science, but more unfortunate in its influence on the social, intellectual, and moral progress of the race.

All the problems that relate to man will not be settled by the present generation, nor within the coming century. We are only in the infancy of those sciences, which are to fully reveal to us man's nature, and the best conditions of his physical, social, and moral development. Thousands of mistakes will be made in Politics, Religion, and Education in all its branches, before our schools will present to us a course of study and discipline that will be what the best good of the world demands. Our railroads, telegraphs, and other inventions and discoveries, will be perfected long before a perfect, or even tolerable, system of education and form of government, will be agreed upon by all men, even when they have the same society to provide for. What can we do in such a chaos of opinion? Little more than to understand that there is chaos, and govern ourselves accordingly. Instead of ruthlessly pulling down what has been done, before our time, simply because there is clamor for change, let it stand till its uselessness or injury is clearly seen,—it will do little harm till then. Instead of undertaking to complete the work, which will take the time, and strength, and wisdom, and suffering, of many generations, let us write upon all our work, "*To be taken away, when better materials and better methods are discovered.*" Let us encourage those who are to come after us, to make progress, by sweeping our work away as soon as its defects are seen. But instead of this, we are likely to be satisfied with a defective structure because it is the work of our own hands, or of those whom we admire, and to pronounce anathemas upon him who shall dare to remove its foundations, or even speak slightingly of its boasted perfections. Thus the influence of a great name has reached down through generations, protecting gross errors that ought to have been swept away—errors that palsied the power of thought, and forbade the growth of man's better nature.

In contrast to this veneration for established error, because it has long passed current for truth, we find those who would sweep from modern life every vestige of the past. Their strength is spent mainly in demolishing; or, if they build at all, it is with wood, and hay, and stubble, hastily gathered and destined soon to perish.

We claim for ourselves no right to entail errors upon those who come after us; nor dare we yet stand idle, for fear of making mistakes. He who waits till he is sure of not making them, will do very little for the world.

When I consider how much still remains unknown,—when I consider the mistakes of the best observers, and the disagreements of those who interpret accepted facts, I can only assure myself that these subjects have been presented as I have read them in nature, and can only hope that the work has been done with due caution. The conclusions are presented as suggestions, whose truth is to be tried by future observers. No one will be more pleased than myself, when these conclusions are displaced by others, which plainly arise from broader and sounder generalizations. But such generalizations can never be reached by those theorists who manufacture their own facts, nor by those observers who have reduced themselves by their narrow fields of labor to the condition of scientific artisans.

To secure the results which all desire,—the full knowledge of man in all his relations,—two classes of laborers are needed; those who give to a single department of Nature, or phase of society, the study of a lifetime, and those who have power to use the labors of such men in forming a system of education or the machinery of government. But the specialist is often tempted to generalize far beyond where he has the ability to go. His success in one department gives him courage to enter fields as a master, where he is only a novice. His acknowledged excellence, in a single department, gives his words weight on subjects of which he is utterly ignorant. So it not unfrequently happens that a learned man does as much mischief by his crude theories on subjects beyond his sphere of knowledge, as he does good by his positive additions to science, in his own proper field of labor. The systematizer, on the other hand, is often so wanting in the power of original observation, and scientific training, and so ignorant of Nature, as to be unable to secure facts for himself or to test and select those fitted for his purpose, when they are supplied by others. He is likely to start with just facts enough of local value to lead him astray in all broad generalizations. He treats of the world as he sees it in one isolated spot, or as he thinks it ought to be. He forms a logical system of science, but when it is carefully tested, Nature disowns it. She has a logic of her own. His theories are without support. The first careful observer points out their defects and they become a mass of rubbish to lumber book-shelves.

There is apparently no help for this state of things in the present condition of science; especially of those departments of science which relate to human life and action.

In Natural science the materials are fast accumulating. We have abroad an army of trained observers far better than the world ever saw before. The means of observing,—the telescopes, microscopes, spectroscopes, and museums, as well as the means of travelling,—are tenfold better than they were a century ago. In one year a man may see more of the earth than Humboldt could see in ten. Give him now Humboldt's power of seeing,—not with the eyes alone, but with the mind,—and how wonderfully have these modern inventions increased his power of observing! Thus, early in life, can now be gathered materials which were utterly beyond the reach of the great masters of the past ages. These facilities are now put to their best use, by a most accurate training of the senses. The whole man has been trained as an observer of nature. In the observing and recording of facts, great accuracy has been secured, so that in the works of our greatest living naturalists, we can, in the majority of cases, implicitly trust their statement of facts, even while dissenting entirely from the conclusions, which they draw from those facts. This is a great step. For although facts are not all,—for facts may lead astray,—yet we must have them. They are the materials with which we are to build. It is a great point to be sure of our materials—to have them in abundance, to be sure that they are sound enough to bear the strain, if they are only put in the right position.

If we could have the facts without the crude theories, which bind them together and too often conceal them, or keep them from their appropriate use,—as brick and stone are wasted in poorly constructed buildings with low ceilings, in gloomy corners, and over cesspools, which bring disease to all that inhabit them,—we should be fortunate. But few men are like David of old, willing to collect materials that others may build wisely and well. The building must go up with crude and scanty materials, according to some hastily-formed plan. Such a building sometimes stands for generations, because some famous man built it, or slept in it; or simply because it has stood so long, that it seems a sort of sacrilege to tear it away! So it is with systems of belief—with theories. They may abound with uncontrovertible facts, but every fact may still be the source of mischief, because misinterpreted. And yet these theories stand because they have some famous names to uphold them.

But let us have faith and patience. The solar system had to wait long before man could see its beauty, from the Sun as centre, and form a true system of Astronomy. Men raged against a true theory of the heavens as infidel and absurd, and clung to their old systems invented by great men. The chemical elements waited longer to have men learn their simple laws of combination, and that bodies become heavier by being burned. Not a century has passed since men believed in phlogiston,—that something escaped from bodies when burning, so that they become lighter,—as some men now believe that when the air is heavy, the smoke falls! Longer still did the earth wait to have her strata counted and measured; and a few of the generation still remain, who believe that the earth is not quite six thousand years older than themselves.

When old notions begin to break up because shown to be false, then men rush to opposite extremes. Then, in the disturbance of the *transition period*, all sorts of crudities appear. The best thing for the overthrow of a bad theory, is that it shall have as many supporters and hard workers in its favor as possible. As a building with poor foundation, and weak materials, and defective workmanship, is sure to fall by its own weight, if built high enough, so a false theory is most readily destroyed, by encouraging its upholders to pile upon it every fact they can accumulate. False theories,—those venerable with age, and those glittering with the polish which genius has just given them,—have their worshippers and admirers.

All these things will right themselves. The generations will die, and the influence of great names is growing less every year. The homes of the great do not stand long in the way of modern progress. I passed along your streets, and saw the crape upon the door, and knew that the great Orator, Statesman, and Scholar slept in the home he had hallowed by his presence,—a home that in other days might have become a shrine. I passed that way again. The home had vanished. Massive walls of stone had taken its place, and the "EVERETT BLOCK" was echoing with the din of trade. So the opinions of the great men of this age must meet the wants of the age, or they cannot stand. The theories that charm the crowd, will stand only as they represent the truth. For it is with truth that men will build to stand. It must be block, and cement, and form. And if man would build for his own wants, and for the world, that which will remain, he must study himself—all his needs—his needs as an animal, as a man, as an individual, as member of society,—and as a worshipper of the Invisible. When all the members of society understand all these things, there will no longer be a repression of instincts as wicked. They will be cultured to their full extent as conditions for higher action. They will be trained in obedience to a will guided by Intellect, and urged on by Obligation. They will be ready, at any moment, to come into action, at any moment to retreat, to lead in the fight, or to support another division. Then will the man be educated, and then, and not till then, will there be as true a theory in every department of Nature, and of human life, as there is now of the Solar System. Then "men will build states and churches as naturally as caterpillars build webs," and for the same reason that they build them now, because their instincts compel them to the work; but then they will build them as wisely as caterpillars build webs, because they will be as truly self-guided by the use of the higher powers, as the caterpillar is wisely guided by the lower instinct, that blindly directs, giving knowledge and skill. Happy will be the thousandth generation, if the moral Instincts and Intellect combined, appropriating all the provisions that have been made for them, shall approach in their uniform results for man, what the lowest instinctive principles to-day, secure for the lowest tribes of creation.

APPENDIX.

A.

NOTE TO TWELFTH LECTURE.

THE conditions under which the Lectures were delivered, made it difficult, if not impossible, to consider the arguments that have been urged against the possession of religious instincts by man, from the time of LOCKE'S war against innate ideas to the present day. A few points from various writers, may enable us to give the doctrine here announced, a fairer presentation, than has been made in the Lecture.

It is not contended, that these instincts or their products, exist in man naturally, in any such sense as the "*innate ideas*" were supposed to exist,—the doctrine of which Locke opposed. What his notion was of that *innate idea of God,* which he denied the existence of, he informs us, B. I. ch. iv., § 17.—"If God had set any impression and character on the understanding of men, it is most reasonable to expect it should have been some *clear and uniform idea* of Himself, as far as our weak capabilities were capable to receive so incomprehensible and infinite object."

Such an idea of God, which should give to man, or be to man, all the knowledge of God which he is capable of securing, no one, certainly, at the present day, would believe to be innate.

What we intend to teach, is that the nature of man is such, that in its developments, the religious instincts which we have mentioned, arise as naturally and as necessarily, *as impulses, and conditions of progress* in the true knowledge of God and of our relations to him, as the animal instincts arise at certain times, as the condition of growth in knowledge by experience. A child may die so young that not one of its appetites, desires or instincts, ever comes into play, that we know of. Do we on that account say, that such a child had none of them? We may say that, because none of them had come into activity, but he had a nature that would surely give rise to them, under the proper conditions for its normal development. They are provided for in the nature of his being ; and that is all we mean to say of the religious instincts. One may be so young, so deficient in original mental power, or so degraded, that these religious instincts have not been called into activity—sufficiently certain, to make any impression on the observer.

The writers who deny the existence of any thing like an innate idea of God, seem almost uniformly to admit, by implication, what seems to us to be proof of the existence in man of these religious *instincts* as we have explained them. And we refer here again to the distinctions drawn in the Tenth Lecture, between *instinctive* and *intuitive* knowledge.

LOCKE in the section from which we have quoted (§ 17) says,—"though the knowledge of a God be the most natural discovery of human Reason, yet the idea of Him is not innate." We do not believe that the idea of a God is *innate,* as Locke used the word "idea," nor in any proper use of that word. But why is it, that "*the knowledge of a God* (should) *be the most natural discovery of the human Reason,*" as Locke admits, unless it be on account of those special impulses and tendencies in man's nature, which we call instincts, that certainly urge him on, and in a measure direct him, so that he may intellectually make the full discovery of that which shall satisfy the yearnings of his being? The knowledge of a God, of which LOCKE speaks, considered abstractly, is not easy at all; and the fact that children receive it so fully as they do, at so early an age, is proof of some special adaptability of the ideas relating to God, to the human mind.

COUSIN, in his examination of LOCKE, has made some good points on this subject, which we may quote, without assenting to all that is implied in the extracts. "*Every thing leads to God,*" says he. And again, "Do not go to consult the savage, the child, the idiot, to know whether they have the idea of God; ask them, *or rather without asking them any thing*, ascertain if they have the idea of the imperfect and the finite ; and if they have it,—and they cannot but have it, if they have the least apperception,—be sure that they have an obscure and confused idea of something infinite and perfect ; *be sure that what they discern of themselves and of the world, does not suffice them, and that they, at once, humble and exalt themselves in an intimate faith in the existence of something infinite and perfect, that is to say, of God.* The *word* may be wanting among them, because the idea is not yet clear and distinct; but no less does it exist within the folds of the opening intelligence, and the philosophic observer easily discovers it there."

Passing many of the able thinkers, who have treated of this subject in some form, as Psychologists simply, we are more interested at present, with the views of those, who have of late treated it, from the broader field of view—Anthropology.

Mr. Darwin, in his "DESCENT OF MAN," published since these Lectures were written, denies that man has naturally the idea of God, but he grants all we claim, when he says, "If, however, we include under the term 'religion' the belief in unseen or spiritual agencies, the case is wholly different, *for this belief* seems *to be almost universal with the less civilized races.*" And the poor Fuegian declared in the most solemn manner, says Mr. Darwin, "Oh, Mr. Boynoe, much rain, much snow, blow much," when he saw Mr. Boynoe, needlessly, as he thought, killing the ducks. And yet Mr. Darwin adds, that he could never discover that the Fuegians believed in what we should call a God! Probably not. Nor is that the question here. The question is whether they had struggling within, an instinct that tended to reveal God, or to lead them to seek for a knowledge of God by all its impulses and tendencies. as other instincts work in man. It took the killing of those ducks to bring out the belief of the Fuegian, in an unseen being who controlled the elements, and in man's accountability to him for his actions.

Sir JOHN LUBBOCK, after presenting his proof against the existence of any knowledge of God, among the degraded tribes of men, considering all their superstitions, expresses this sentiment, which is quoted approvingly by Darwin, and commented upon by him, as follows: "'*It is not too much to say that the horrible dread of unknown evil hangs like a thick cloud over savage life, and embitters every pleasure.*' These miserable and indirect consequences of our highest faculties, may be compared with the incidental and occasional mistakes of the instincts of the lower animals." To all this we agree, only substituting *religious instincts* for "highest faculties," and add that the mistakes of these, are more terrible than those of the lower instincts, because they are higher, and are linked in their activity, with all of man's highest powers. They struggle, but they need light and guidance, which must come to them, through the comprehending powers, from the Revelations in God's works and Word.

THE END.

www.ingramcontent.com/pod-product-compliance
Lightning Source LLC
LaVergne TN
LVHW010541100826
845148LV00001B/259

9781425576295